"Knaus's original book *Overcoming Procrastination* has helped thou. people dealing with this endemic problem of delaying tasks in their personal and professional lives, causing them endless hours of anxiety and possibly depression. This latest workbook not only incorporates those timeless principles of overcoming procrastination but adds excellent exercises to reinforce their learning. The action plans help individuals integrate their learning for lasting results. Everyone could use this book."

> —Dominic DiMattia, Ed.D., Executive Director,
> Albert Ellis Institute

"In introducing his ideas, Knaus takes us back over a century in psychology, quoting William James: 'By changing our thinking, we can change our lives.' We've certainly known this for a long time, but it is in the individual realization of this simple truth that we can enhance our well being. This procrastination workbook provides a useful tool for readers who are actively engaged in the challenging process of self-change and are ready to change their lives through changing their thinking about procrastination."

> —Timothy A. Pychyl, Ph.D., Associate Professor,
> Psychology, Carleton University, Ottawa

"Procrastinators need all the help they can get, especially in maintaining progress toward overcoming what is a rather common phenomenon. *The Procrastination Workbook* is a valuable resource for those seeking to change. It is a great contribution at both the conceptual and applied levels. It is a valuable resource for mental health professionals and those of their clients who are procrastinators."

> —Stephen G. Weinrach, Ph.D., Professor, Villanova
> University

"Although this self-help guide to procrastination cessation has a serious purpose, it is amazingly entertaining. Rife with amusing and illuminating quotes, quips, and anecdotes, the medicine goes down easily and one is propelled on a wave of enthusiasm and zeal into a new groove by a host of thoughtful, pragmatic exercises."

> —Joseph Gerstein, MD, Assistant Clinical Professor
> of Medicine, Harvard Medical School

"Bill Knaus tells us that when we procrastinate, we take unwanted tasks and drag them through the present and into the future. In a delightful way, this workbook tells how to unburden your tomorrows from these procrastination sorrows and find ways to truly enjoy your life. Buy the book and start today!"

> —Richard C. Sprinthall, Ph.D., Director of Graduate
> Studies, American International College

THE Procrastination
WORKBOOK

Your Personalized

Program for

Breaking Free

from the Patterns

That Hold You Back

William Knaus, Ed.D.

Foreword by
Albert Ellis, Ph.D.

New Harbinger Publications, Inc.

Publisher's Note

This publication is designed to provide accurate and authoritative information in regard to the subject matter covered. It is sold with the understanding that the publisher is not engaged in rendering psychological, financial, legal, or other professional services. If expert assistance or counseling is needed, the services of a competent professional should be sought.

Distributed in Canada by Raincoast Books

Copyright © 2002 by William Knaus
                New Harbinger Publications, Inc.
                5674 Shattuck Avenue
                Oakland, CA 94609

Cover design by Poulson/Gluck Designs
Text design by Michele Waters

ISBN-10 1-57224-295-7
ISBN-13 978-1-57224-295-1

Printed in the United States of America

New Harbinger Publications' website address: www.newharbinger.com

11   10   09

15   14   13   12   11   10

FSC
Mixed Sources
Product group from well-managed
forests and other controlled sources

Cert no. SW-COC-002283
www.fsc.org
© 1996 Forest Stewardship Council

Contents

Foreword

As I happily remember my first association with Bill Knaus, I am still surprised to recall that it was when he was in graduate school at the University of Tennessee in 1965. He came to one of my workshops in Rational Emotive Behavior Therapy (REBT), and I was amazed that he seemed to grasp the essence of this form of psychotherapy with remarkable acuity and ability. I concluded at that time that he was both born and raised with an unusual tendency to think rationally. How right I was! Shortly afterward, Bill became one of the training fellows of the Albert Ellis Institute in New York—and, once again, proved to be one of the outstanding practitioners of REBT that the institute has certified.

Since 1968, Bill has not only ably practiced REBT with many clients and with a good many business, educational, and other organizations, but he has also written extensively about its use in a number of important areas. He has pioneered in writing with *Rational Emotive Education*, the first book to apply REBT approach to teachers and educators. He especially fostered the REBT approach to procrastination in the early 1970s by writing a pamphlet and taping a cassette recording both entitled *Overcoming Procrastination*, which have been bestsellers since that time. In 1977 he joined me in writing the first major book, again entitled *Overcoming Procrastination*, which has been in print with New American Library since that time and is one of their fastest-selling titles ever.

After writing several other books and pamphlets on the Rational Emotive Behavior Therapy approach to a number of other fields, Bill has very ably summed up many of his main contributions to self-help therapy by writing *The Procrastination Workbook*. This is an outstanding contribution for people who want to work effectively on what Bill wisely calls the *Do It Now* philosophy. It beautifully shows its readers how to stop delaying and interfering with their lives in several crucial areas—personal, family, social, school, and work areas.

The Procrastination Workbook, like Bill's other excellent self-help books, is written in an exceptionally lucid and readable style, includes many thinking, feeling, and behavioral exercises, and is practical and hardheaded as any book could be. Don't procrastinate! Read this book *now* and really discover how to apply its host of very useful self-management methods, so that they appreciably add to your happiness, health, and effective living *now!*

> Albert Ellis, Ph.D., President
> Albert Ellis Institute

Introduction

Upon hearing the word *"procrastination,"* you might imagine a pile of unpaid bills, a disorganized closet, an extension form for taxes that were due on April 15, people showing up late, an expired auto-inspection sticker, or telling yourself that you will respond to an emergent priority, such as returning a phone call, then forgetting to follow through. These examples of missing deadlines, rushing to meet them at the eleventh hour, or pushing them off until you remember to do them are classic examples of procrastination. Often the more common form of procrastination involves activities that you want to do or think are beneficial, such as taking on a new hobby, exercising more, or facing an inhibition or fear. Because these personal-development challenges are "just about you," they often lay fallow.

Whether handicapping or troublesome, few escape the perils of procrastination. Persistent forms of procrastination are serious problems for hundreds of millions. Perhaps as many as 90 percent of the U.S. population has at least one area (and probably more) where they feel stumped by procrastination (Ellis and Knaus 1979). Procrastination research psychologists Jesse Harriot and Joseph Ferrari (1996) estimate that 20 percent are afflicted with an invasive, handicapping, chronic variety of procrastination. Even top executives fritter time in aimless ways, such as busy work, postponing important decisions, avoiding uncomfortable priority situations, checking their stock portfolios several times an hour, phoning acquaintances, attending to business unrelated to the organization, or engaging in senseless squabbling. Sixty percent of college students consider procrastination a habit serious enough to require help in overcoming it. Regardless of your age or role in life, it is the persistent, pressured form of procrastination urges and distractions that merit close attention and special efforts to contain. Fortunately, there is a great deal you can do to curb your procrastination impulses, to take charge of your life, and to advance your positive values and interests.

Procrastination is one of those equal-opportunity afflictions that can strike anywhere, at any level and at any stage of your life. People who procrastinate come from everywhere, including every walk of life and occupation. We catch children in the act of procrastinating when they say, "Not now, Mom." Retirees without specific plans easily procrastinate their time away. Truly, few go through life without experiencing the effects of procrastination.

Delays on meeting deadlines are the tip of a titanic procrastination iceberg. Beneath the surface, you can find a broad range of maintenance and personal development delays that also can prove chilling and painfully limiting. What we'll call "maintenance procrastination" involves such matters as letting your environment fill with needless clutter. "Personal procrastination" includes putting off dealing with anxiety, delaying on starting a weight-loss program, or doing a hesitation waltz when you want to approach someone whom you find attractive. These personal-development forms of procrastination occur when we think we have all the time in the world to address a general development issue, stretching that opportunity too far into the future. For example, you want to lose weight—but not right now. Perhaps after the holidays you'll start. Then after the holidays, you find another reason to delay. Deadline, maintenance, and personal-development delays are mainly self-handicapping. Some can have broader social implications, such as when delays hinder others.

Postponing paying bills and putting off coping with, say, a fear of rejection come from the same desire to avoid fear, discomfort, tedium, boredom, or some other negative emotion or sensation. Although some activities you face will be truly unpleasant, a big advantage in getting them over with is to decrease the time you feel hassled by them.

Each form of procrastination typically includes a "mañana illusion," where we filter reality through a false hope that the delay won't hurt anyone and the future will be better because we can later control what we delay today. In the world of the consummate procrastinator, this rarely happens. For example, in deadline procrastination you hope to bypass the calendar and the clock. When the clock runs out, you pay a penalty, get an extension, or get off the hook. Living amidst an avalanche of maintenance delay situations, you will have many stressful reminders of what lies undone, and, perhaps, dreams of better days to come. When you stress yourself with these delays you can distract yourself from thinking clearly and creatively.

You are likely to find procrastination as a component in major emotional disorders, such as anxiety and depression, and in substance-abuse disorders. Once you stop procrastinating on these challenges, you can concentrate your efforts on resolving them. Otherwise, you'll have to trust that some happy accident will vanquish the problem, or that you will "grow out of it."

Ready, Set, Go

Join me on an adventure of exploring procrastination. In this challenging venture, you are the pilot. You choose the destination and how you will get there. It's your life. Whatever the outcome, you may discover that the process is even more exciting than the results that you achieve.

Throughout *The Procrastination Workbook*, you'll find basic and advanced ideas, exercises, and techniques to support you in overcoming procrastination. Part of the process involves educating yourself about procrastination and about your options and choices. Another part involves isolating an area where you procrastinate, then observing, studying, tinkering with, adjusting, testing, retesting, and refining your ability to override the habit with a proactive one. The exercises and techniques assist you in this cause.

To help you organize your efforts, I've broken this workbook down into two parts. The first is a basic program for curbing procrastination. The second includes advanced and special-interest topics. In both parts, I describe dimensions and dynamics of procrastination to help you to demystify the process. This self-education phase is an important staging ground for making changes from procrastination to proactive reactions.

It's important to read the chapters in their order. Later chapters draw information from the preliminary chapters. Through engaging in this learning process, you will build on a coordinated series of information-recording exercises and practical problem-solving techniques designed to help you curb procrastination.

The information-recording sections are a way to collect specific information about what happens when you procrastinate. You will be using the information you record in the first five chapters to help create a master five-step program in chapter 6. For example, in chapter 1, you'll start a procrastination log exercise that you will use to generate personal information about the procrastination zones you find most troublesome. You can roll information from the log over to successive chapters, but since the log is also ongoing, I suspect that this effort will help refine your understanding of procrastination and the ways to curb or contain procrastination messages and activities. Working from your own personal data, you will create the counterprocrastination plans that will generate your program, tailored to you. You will find many guidelines to help you in this quest.

The practical techniques are for dealing with both general and specific procrastination challenges. For example, you'll learn over 100 techniques that range from time management to disputing procrastination thinking. It is unrealistic to test all the separate techniques you read about in this workbook. Begin with one or a few techniques that you can and will do. Practice them until they become routine. Then add others that seem promising.

A Thought for a Start

Within these pages you will find many ways to look at procrastination, and you will discover a broad range of solutions. You'll have many options and choices. The idea is for you to use what you can to create opportunities for yourself to take greater charge of your own life. Beyond the practical results that you create for yourself, you may find the most valued part of curbing procrastination is your growing sense of competency and self-mastery.

The satisfaction that comes from containing procrastination-related hassles can lead to a sense of personal competency that comes from within. In that sense, this book is like a set of tools and sample designs that you can use to shape a more powerful you. You are the artist. You do the creating.

Coping with procrastination takes work and time, but perhaps no more than the time you would set aside for taking a few academic courses. In this sense, it's amazing how many people spend significant amounts of time to get a good grade in a course and expend comparatively little time and effort developing their personal strengths. It's almost as though they say, "I can wait. A history course is more important."

Would you be willing to put as much time and effort into dealing with procrastination as you would spend reading, studying, and participating in a history course? If you did expend about the same time and effort on procrastination, the chances are that you would make observable progress—turning procrastination into a rascal in retreat.

Dealing with procrastination is a lifetime challenge to those who seek better ways to enjoy their lives. Every day you can learn new ways to support your efforts to cope with your procrastination-habit urges and impulses and to make welcomed progress. In the meantime, psychologists are learning more about procrastination and how to beat it. Indeed, procrastination is such an important matter for the millions who want to kick this challenging habit that research is exploding in this area. DePaul University psychologist Dr. Joseph Ferrari and Carleton University (Ottawa) psychologist Dr. Timothy Pychyl (2000) edited a special issue on procrastination for the *Journal of Social Behavior and Personality* that quickly became a modern classic on this ageless topic. Although understanding and dealing with procrastination continues as a work in process, *The Procrastination Workbook* will give you powerful ideas, exercises, and techniques to use to curb the procrastination behemoth that dwells within. When you get this factor out of your life you'll have more time for the joy you can experience through executing accomplishments.

PART I

Basic Ways to Get Things Done

CHAPTER 1

Procrastination Machinations

I am procrastination. I come in different guises. I am sometimes obvious. I am sometimes hidden. But I am always there, lurking, waiting, preparing to crash into your life at any moment when you are vulnerable. I hold power over your life. When you flee from me, you strengthen me. Even if you vanquish me for a while, I'll come back when you are least aware. I have the power to befuddle your life again and again.

Does this sound familiar? If so, you are not alone. Procrastination is a part of life. *Everybody* does it. Many people put things off until tomorrow, and when tomorrow comes, they put them off until the next tomorrow. The idea that later is better is a common illusion behind this "tomorrow outlook." When tomorrow comes, the pattern resurfaces, and we excuse ourselves by promising that we'll later reform and act with volition. But no time for that now, we tell ourselves. After all, there is always tomorrow. We'll deal with procrastination then.

People have been playing on the same procrastination theme since the dawning of cultural history. We see these traces everywhere. The ancient Babylonian King Hammurabi incorporated an antiprocrastination measure into his 283 laws by setting a deadline for making a complaint. The ancient Romans gave us the derivatives of the word *procrastination*, which means to push forward until tomorrow. Two-thousand years ago, the Roman Emperor Marcus Aurelius cautioned against needless delays. The eighteenth-century English philosopher, Thomas Hobbes, defined personal worth as one's ability to contribute, and, thus, to use time effectively. Over the millennium, folk sayings convey a message about the value of avoiding needless delays. "A stitch in time saves nine" directs us to tarry not, lest we create a bigger problem for ourselves. And just as procrastination has spread over the past millennium, two-thousand years from now I'd bet that we'd still find people struggling to contain their procrastination tendencies.

What Is This Thing We Call Procrastination?

The word *procrastination* comes from the Latin *pro*, which means "forward," and *crastinate*, which means "tomorrow." But as practically everyone knows, this tomorrow process can be a big snag.

The power of procrastination erupts deeply from within. It often masquerades as a friend. "Let it wait," we hear ourselves say, "for when you feel rested, you'll fly through these tasks to create a tomorrow that all can envy." This is one of those procrastination paradoxes, where a soothing idea has hidden barbs. You feel relief when you think you can later gain command over what you currently don't want to do. The barb is found in practicing a negative pattern of retreat.

When you procrastinate you needlessly postpone, delay, or put off a relevant activity until another day or time. When you procrastinate, you *always* substitute an alternative activity for the relevant one (Knaus 2000). The alternative activity may be almost as timely or important as the one you put off. But more likely, it will be irrelevant, such as daydreaming instead of writing a report.

There are procrastination acts and procrastination patterns. "Procrastination acts" are random. You postpone returning a library book until after it's overdue. You finished the book. But you don't want to go out of your way to return it on time. This is an isolated occurrence, since you typically promptly return what you borrow. Procrastination patterns are consistent, predictable habits of delay that may not always occur in the same situation, but follow an identifiable sequence. This sequence often begins with feeling discomfort about an activity, and then "mindlessly" shifting to a secondary or irrelevant one (Knaus 1982).

Procrastination varies in its magnitude of seriousness. The process exists on a continuum where some things you postpone doing are trivial and bear no notable cost. You put aside magazines you want to read, and you are the only one who knows or cares. At the extreme, procrastination can generalize to many important facets of your existence and diminishes the quality of your life. You are out of work, afraid to go for an interview, you procrastinate on dealing with your fear and settle for the first job that takes the least amount of interviewing strain. At a general procrastination level, you can find yourself in a whirlpool of worry as you habitually put off so many activities that it becomes difficult to keep count.

A Basic Two-Stage Process

Procrastination can be a case of pure avoidance. But most often, procrastination minimally involves a two-stage process. The first part involves an impulse to delay. That impulse can be triggered by a negative mood, a threat, discomfort, anticipated tedium, or some other real or imagined negative condition. The second stage almost immediately

> Procrastination is the art of making something into more
> than it is, until it expands into more than it needs to be.

blends with the first. You reassure yourself that later is better, such as when you delay by telling yourself that you just need to warm up, and then you'll get control of the situation. Then you wait to warm up.

In this two-stage process, procrastination has both an active and a passive phase. The active phase of procrastination involves engaging in avoidance activities such as napping or daydreaming instead of finishing a pressing report. The passive process involves excuse making and false justifications, such as deciding that tomorrow is a better time to start, coming up with excuses like "time just ran out." Both the active and passive processes involve busywork that can vastly exceed the time and effort needed to finish the delayed activity. Procrastinators are also likely to obfuscate by using the passive verb tenses with "is" and "was" to excuse their delay, thus making this active-passive process more complex. "Mistakes were made," for example, is a classic passive obfuscation.

When you distract yourself from a priority activity, you can temporarily avoid haggling with yourself over what you view as a hassle. For example, you might feel a twinge of discomfort as you anticipate the unpleasant aspects of phoning a merchant to cancel an order. You haggle with yourself about whether or not to get the call out of the way. You might then switch to thinking about the future where your mood might improve or where you believe you will feel better prepared to deal with possible merchant objections. Weeks later, while still contemplating a potential conflict, the unwanted merchandise arrives. You now have another series of decisions to make, including going through the added inconvenience of returning the merchandise or keeping what you don't want, perhaps rationalizing that you may find it useful someday.

What Is Relevant?

The American inventor, scientist, and diplomat Ben Franklin (1989) set as his life goal the task of achieving a variety of virtues. He said, "Resolve to perform what you ought. Perform without fail what you resolve." But Franklin had to admit that he fell far short of the mark of his resolve to keep things in their place. However, Franklin's historical accomplishments are what we remember him by, not whether he knew where he put his quill pen. Would we call Franklin a procrastinator because he fell short of one of his development goals? To what extent was that goal relevant compared to his other work, such as discovering electricity?

Procrastination involves delaying or postponing a timely and relevant activity until another time or place. But who decides what is purposeful or relevant? The government says you must file your taxes by April 15. That's relevant because they have the power to punish your delays with penalties. But what is relevant and urgent for one person may have little value for another, especially when actions are discretionary. Say that your mate has an agenda of things for you to do and asks you to stop what you're doing to attend to their list. Are you procrastinating if you put off your mate's to-do list? Your mate may feel that you absolutely are. You may feel differently.

People can define themselves as procrastinating when, in fact, they operate effectively. If you think you're a procrastinator yet routinely follow through and reliably meet deadlines, the issue may be one of expectations. Suppose you expect of yourself that you will operate with perfect consistency or like a perpetual-motion machine. Although you briskly follow through, you find yourself only 99 percent efficient. This would be like efficiency paradise for most. But when you over-focus on that 1 percent delay rate and view yourself as having failed in your quest for perfect efficiency, the relevant issue is perfectionism.

Not all delays are procrastination examples. Strategic delays were known as far back as the ancient world. In *The Odyssey*, the ancient Greek poet Homer (1992) described a now-famous fictional strategic delay. Circa 800 B.C. the blind poet told the story of Ulysses, who went to fight in the Trojan War. After the war was won, the god Poseidon sent Ulysses on a ten-year odyssey. In the meanwhile, suitors besieged Ulysses' wife, Penelope. Upon invading her home and eating her food, they pressured her to choose one among them to marry. Not knowing if Ulysses was alive or dead, Penelope conceived of a plan to delay a decision. She persuaded the suitors to wait until she finished weaving a shroud. So, during the daytime she sat before a great loom to weave long threads. At night she unraveled what she had done. About four years later, the suitors caught on. But before the shroud was finally done, Ulysses returned.

Strategic delays are relevant in other ways. A slower pace can make sense as you proceed into areas of uncertainty where you need to learn as you go in order to gain clarity. Facing situations where you deliberately have to figure out what information you will need, impulsive actions may appear decisive yet prove costly. Say you need a new car to replace the one you have that is beyond repair. So instead of immediately visiting the closest automobile dealer and paying list price, you do some research. What brand and models best fit your current needs? What cars have the best frequency of repair figures? Is the vehicle crash-worthy? What are the best cars for fuel economy? What is the best potential deal you're likely to make? This type of strategic delay is preferable to an impulse purchase, which, by the way, might be viewed as procrastinating on making a quality decision.

How Procrastination Can Affect You

Lost personal-development opportunities are far different from the deadline stuff, such as buying an airline ticket in advance of a trip or returning a library book before it is overdue. Sure, performing effectively in these areas can bring a sense that you are in control of what you do. These activities are important. But often we find that the moments we fritter away when we're supposed to be working on our personal development often extend into feelings of failure and loss.

When this habit generalizes, you can find that you put off many activities you previously relished. You lose contact with good friends. The tools for your favorite hobby gather dust. A procrastination habit develops, the time and effort you put into busy work, sidetracking yourself, or making excuses can gobble time from valued leisure activities that you previously enjoyed.

What we do in the present is a powerful propellant for what's to come and what will linger undone. In a very sad way, precious moments in our lives drift into oblivion when we needlessly delay those things that are important for us to do. It's not that letting dishes pile up in the kitchen sink, by itself, is so important that it will damper your daily delights. Nor will letting clutter pile up in your closet, by itself, stop you from getting a promotion at work. But when it is important to you to keep up with your activities of daily living, and these maintenance delays pile up, you can sense the power of procrastination crushing down on your life. You want to write a novel, but put off the research. You think you can make a difference by running for state representative, but the deadline passes, and along with it, your dream. When procrastination rushes before reason, losses mark the boundaries of a graveyard for missed opportunities.

A Complex Problem

Procrastination (like any entrenched and interactive thinking, feeling, and action-habit pattern) has many nuances that can easily slip beneath the radar of even the most astute self-observers. It can represent a symptom of discomfort fears, self-doubts, perfectionism, fear of failure, risk aversion, anxiety, rebellion, depression, or feeling vulnerable. It can start from anticipating or judging that an activity is too complicated, troublesome, fearsome, or boring to do. Procrastination can emerge at the level of perception where our sensory impressions go to our higher mental processes but first and more directly to stimulate memories associated with negative emotions. For example, you feel inhibited, recoil from meeting new people, and put off dealing with social situations because of the strong negative emotions you experience.

Whether procrastination thinking or avoidance impulses stir from pre-set beliefs or from perceptually driven negative memories, these conditions typically blend. But regardless of the reasons for procrastinating, the nexus of this learned habit lies in avoidance through diversionary activities. If procrastination did not have these distinctive features, there would be no common ground for us to meet the procrastination challenge. Since there is a common ground, we can devise many ways to break the habit.

Our needless delays may not occur in the same way or with consistency. You may sometimes follow through effectively on something like completing an investigative report, then later give lame excuses to justify an overdue financial report. On a very good day, when your mood is upbeat and you think you can handle anything that comes your way, you might be an efficiency superstar and complete detailed tasks that you would normally delay. For a brief time, you may believe you have permanently whipped procrastination. But when tomorrow comes and your mood changes, you discover, to your chagrin, that you are back to the same delaying ways. What a baffling experience! But these varying efficiency experiences show how mood and mind connect. The thoughts you *think* affect the way you feel and your mood can affect the way you think. The very optimistic news is that by changing your mind-set, you may be able to change your mood. And whether or not you improve your mood, there is much you can do to boost your effectiveness—which can, as a by-product, result in a good mood.

You can procrastinate for various reasons and produce different outcomes. Some people procrastinate because they don't want to do something and suffer no illusions that they may pay a price for the delay. Others want to escape the discomfort they feel while in the process of doing something they don't like to do. So they stop as soon as they are able, then find ways to delay. At other times, you may avoid something you don't want to do and justify the delay by telling yourself something vague, such as, "I'm just not ready." You may date people who aren't what you really want to avoid getting emotionally attached. You might also resist imposed chores and duck the problem by complaining of fatigue. These differences show varied reasons for procrastination and can make the solutions for procrastination seem daunting. But there is a simple solution to procrastination and we'll take that up next.

A Simple, but Challenging, Solution

A solution to overcoming procrastination is to simply *do it now*. This means, getting reasonable things done in a reasonable way within a reasonable time in order to increase your personal efficiency, effectiveness, and satisfaction with living. But what is simple to say is not always so easy to do. Implementing this solution can be challenging.

Though it's a challenge for most of us, learning to shed procrastination barriers can bring you closer to where you truly feel in charge of your life. And while procrastination is rarely overcome by decree, the process of gaining mastery over procrastination is not as toilsome as it first seems. While radical changes are possible, most sustainable changes occur through small steps and by degree. Small steps by themselves are sometimes hard to individually quantify, yet collectively they yield real progress.

The "First-Things-First Question" is one of those small steps that orient you toward what is most pressing and important to do. In using this question, you ask yourself, "Is there something else that is more timely and important than what I am now doing?" The First-Things-First sets the stage for action against procrastination.

We daily face single situations that we can do on the spot but that we put off. You get a phone call and think you'll get to it later because it will take too much time now. Should you trust your memory? Psychologist David Schacter (2001) notes that with the passage of time your memory can lead you astray. You can readily distort messages, forget important factors, and possibly dwell on what you want to forget. To curb isolated procrastination acts that involve remembering what you can readily forget, use the "Do-It-When-You-First-Can Method." This can save you time and boost your organizing effectiveness. For example, postponing what you can do now frequently leads to future frustrations, such as when you try to relocate misplaced written materials or forget where you put a scrap of paper with an important phone number. Adding time for these searches can ferment into a mental vinegar as you compound your sense of frustration. Developing the Do-It-When-You-First-Can habit is a wiser alternative than doing it whenever you can, or trusting to memory, expecting that important materials won't get lost.

Among those small steps, here is one of the very best. Use the Five-Minute Method to ease yourself into the *do it now* process. Begin by first committing five minutes to start the task or project you're tempted to avoid. Schedule the first step of the task—then do it! At the end of that five-minute period, you decide if you are going to continue for another five minutes. You follow this pattern until you decide to quit or are done. If you decide to quit before you're done, take five minutes to set up what you will do to get a jump on the task when next you begin. Although you only commit to brief work periods, this can be a surprisingly effective way to break a procrastination pattern.

Beware the "Just Do It" Myth

The main idea for dealing with procrastination is to do what you put off. But in the world of those who procrastinate, "just do it" can prove especially deceiving and unrealistic. If you could unwaveringly follow this advice, you wouldn't be reading this workbook.

"Just do it" sounds good in theory. The slogan does offer a solution. But this advice is rarely sufficient to shift from a procrastination habit to one of getting reasonable things done without undue delay. To make the slogan work for you, at the least you'll have to talk yourself through the paces time and time again.

When "just do it" advice goes against a procrastination habit, the habit is usually the victor. The exceptions are when someone in a powerful position tells you to just do it *or else.* In that case, you're more likely to follow through. Otherwise repeating a "just do it" mantra is likely to have the same value the "just say no" commercials for curbing drug abuse among kids and teens. They typically have a zero to negative impact.

Because procrastination involves so many complex features, the best prediction is that "just do it" slogans are interesting for the back of a T-shirt, but not much else.

A Choice Paradox

To procrastinate, all it takes is to substitute a lower priority activity for a timely, relevant, or more important one. To stop procrastinating, all it takes is to do the priority before anything else. Does this make procrastination a choice? Yes, but not necessarily a clear choice. Even when you can see the options, you may still feel like the proverbial moth drawn to a flame.

Procrastination is rarely a pure and uncontaminated choice. If procrastination were a free choice, you could end procrastination now. You tell yourself that stopping procrastination is an act of responsibility. You would decide to stop procrastinating, and you would permanently stop. Such a planless decision to stop procrastinating is more like telling yourself to stop hearing a song playing in your mind, then snapping your fingers and terminating the tune. The melody is likely to drone on and, unlike procrastination, will eventually fade away for other reasons.

As practically everyone who struggles with this p-factor knows, this ancient nemesis follows a seductive habit path that rarely stops without persistent and strongly guided self-directives to act without undue delay. Choice starts to come in to play when you decide to put an end to procrastination, have a good plan, then take the first step to emphasize your intent.

Self-Regulation Training

Procrastination involves a breakdown in our ability to regulate our thoughts and efforts to achieve purposeful, longer-term outcomes. This breakdown starts when you perceive negativity or unpleasantness in all or some aspects of an upcoming priority. Then you substitute another activity with the expectation that you will do better later. This rhythm of delay then continues, even when you know that you would gain more by acting sooner.

Stanford professor and psychologist Albert Bandura uses the concept of self-efficacy to illustrate a self-regulatory direction to follow to take charge of your life. Self-efficacy is the belief that you have the power to organize, regulate, and direct your actions to achieve mastery. With high self-efficacy, you'll predictably procrastinate less. With low self-efficacy, you are likely to procrastinate more.

Among self-regulation methods, the PURRRR acronym describes a six-step—pause utilize, reflect, reason, respond, and revise—process to keep your *do it now* engine purring. You can use this self-regulation direction anytime you are faced with a procrastination situation.

PURRRR

1. Delay the procrastination process by putting it on *pause*. This is the first sign that you intend to establish control over procrastination. But what if you catch yourself overlooking pause? A reminder system can help. You can wear an elastic band on your wrist or mark a green dot on your watch or fingernail to symbolizes "pause." When you see the dot, you remind yourself to pause.

2. The second step involves halting your initial procrastination actions. Here you *utilize* your resources to resist and subdue your procrastination actions. You already subdue impulsive actions every day. Suppose you are in a hurry and come to a red light at a busy intersection. You utilize your common sense to stop at the light rather than risk a crash.

3. The first and second steps set the stage for you to *reflect* on what you are imagining, telling yourself, or picturing in your mind's eye when you feel the urge to procrastinate. In this reflective phase you gather information by reflecting upon the situation, how you feel, what you first tell yourself when you are in a procrastination mode, and what you continue to tell yourself to justify procrastinating.

4. Through reflection, you may already have started to think about your thinking. But in the *reasoning* phase, you take this a step further. You evaluate your procrastination self-talk. For example, anything you tell yourself to needlessly delay is procrastination thinking. Once you evaluate this diversionary trick as misleading thinking, you are less likely to go in a procrastination direction while uttering optimistic fictions disguised as rationality.

5. Following reason, *respond* by mapping steps to crack through your procrastination barriers. Think about the steps that you can take first, or now. There is practically always one part of a challenge that you can start immediately. In this process, give yourself instructions about how to proceed in a *do it now* direction. Then follow your plan by talking and walking yourself through the paces.

6. Reasoning and responding are like sighting along and releasing an arrow. *Revising* is an adjustment phase. Here you look at the results of your actions and adjust your aim and method. Reason is rarely perfect at the start. You can get new ideas. Something you hadn't thought about could happen. If you've overlooked a step, revision involves adding the missing step.

Using the PURRRR mapping process, you put a very challenging procrastination condition into perspective, position yourself for action, act, and adjust what you do to achieve your purposeful objective. Let's look at an example of how PURRRR works. Suppose you feel a strong urge to procrastinate on setting up a dental appointment. You know you have a few cavities but don't want to hassle yourself by calling for an appointment, traveling to the dentist's office, getting an examination, and then rescheduling yourself for the uncomfortable process of getting the cavities drilled and filled. On the other hand, you remember your last toothache, and you have a competing desire to act promptly to prevent a recurrence.

As you think about looking up your dentist's phone number, you suddenly have an unchecked desire to read your favorite magazine. You decide to use PURRRR instead.

1. You *pause* and remind yourself that your first goal is to get the phone number and make the call.

2. You *utilize* your forward-looking capability to resist and subdue your urge to pick up the magazine. This suppression is an act of free will to support the choice to delay your procrastination actions.

3. You *reflect* on what you are telling yourself about setting up the appointment. You hear yourself say that phoning is a hassle because you'll get put on hold and

you won't be able to get a convenient appointment time. Perhaps it is better to phone the following morning.

4. Not willing to accept that hogwash, you *reason* it out. You judge that what you've told yourself is a delay tactic. You remind yourself that your goal is not to avoid a hassle, rather to get something important done. To put teeth into this proactive direction, you ask yourself why you are so optimistic about tomorrow being a better day. Based on your answer, you decide to make the call now.

5. Although you know what to do to make the call, you take an extra minute to map out the steps to make the appointment. You do this to give yourself practice in replacing procrastination thinking with purposeful instructions and actions. You *respond* by first giving yourself verbal instructions. You tell yourself that you will walk to the phone book, open it to the yellow pages under dentist, look up your dentist's number, pick up the phone, dial the number, and set up the appointment. Then you respond in a step-by-step manner according to the instructions.

6. *Revision* comes into play in this way. When you get to the phone, you notice your favorite magazine and some old paperwork. You start to shuffle the papers to see what they are. Then you start to leaf through the magazine. You recognize this as an automatic procrastination ploy and adjust your plan by telling yourself you'll reward yourself by reading the magazine only after you've set up the appointment. You dial the number, set the appointment, then reward yourself by reading your favorite magazine.

Through your self-regulating actions, you develop an increased sense of personal command. As you regulate your actions to gain progressive mastery over procrastination, you are likely to improve the timing and pacing of your actions. You are less likely to feel whipsawed by a habit of delays, and you are more likely to experience the benefits of forward momentum. You also are likely to improve in self-efficacy. PURRRR is a basic way to get started on this self-regulation process and to gain those benefits. Try PURRRR the next time you feel tempted to procrastinate. You can use the following chart to help guide you through the steps.

PURRRR Plan

Procrastination situation: _____.

Pause	Utilize	Reflect	Reason	Respond	Revise
Stop	Resist	Think about what's happening	Think it through	Put yourself through the paces	Make adjustments

Even when you are highly motivated to use PURRRR, you're unlikely to bat 1000. Progress normally comes in increments, sometimes with a breakthrough in a particular area. But imagine if you could improve 10 percent over the next six months, then 10 percent more over the next six months, and continue to find ways to make gains? You will have engaged a process of progressive mastery over needless delays and demonstrated your ability to regulate your efforts toward a positive result. You can assign the change you make to your own efforts rather than to medication, the fates, or luck.

Log It

We rarely monitor the way we go about evaluating, judging, deciding, believing, misperceiving, and so forth. In fact, most of us do a poor job in this area. In the grips of procrastination thinking, it's easy to miss nuances and intricacies such as the images and sensations associated with procrastinating. For this reason, procrastination perceptions and thinking often go unobserved unless we consciously watch for them. Monitoring our thinking is termed *meta cognition*. This is a powerful way to figure out what is happening when we procrastinate.

Psychologists John Borgh and Tanya Chartrand (1999) report that much of what we do in our daily lives involves automatic processing that does the lion's share of our self-regulatory activities. The psychologists go on to say that consciously regulating our thinking and behavior takes effort. This view is useful to underscore. It supports the use of a procrastination log. Logging your experiences gives you recorded information that can aid this self-monitoring as well as provide information you can use throughout this workbook.

Procrastination-log exercises have been used by thousands who profited by having a running, written review of their procrastination practices. It is a surprisingly effective way to slow down the automatic procrastination processes so that you can better understand what you think, feel, and do when you follow a procrastination direction. Once the procrastination process is visible, it is more amenable to evaluation and change.

The log serves multiple purposes. You will be able to use it to jog your memory for what you've accomplished and how you did it. At times, you may reach points where you feel discouraged. Reading a log that shows where you have been and what you have accomplished can help rekindle optimism. Your own words can send the message that you have the ability to build coping skills. The log will also help you to track your progress.

How can you write the log? Some of my clients have used their procrastination logs as a running commentary on their lives, much like you would write a journal or a diary. Through this method, they develop a record of where they've acted without delay, how they did this, and what resulted. They also have concrete examples of where they waylaid themselves through delays, how this happened, and what resulted. There are many ways to do this. Some focus on procrastination situations and list their beliefs, emotions, and behaviors. They then use this information to reflect upon, reason about, and respond effectively against these patterns. Whatever approach you take, the procrastination log will give you a picture of your procrastination habits and progress.

Here is a good way to begin making log entries. To get a good start on collecting useful information about how and why you procrastinate, break down the process to map out what you did about your procrastination episodes throughout each day. If recording every episode seems overwhelming, choose one or two prominent examples each day. To create your own log:

1. Describe the activity you put off

2. What were you feeling when you first acted to delay?

3. What were you thinking when you first began to delay?

4. What did you tell yourself to keep procrastinating on this activity?

5. What was the outcome?

Once you map out what you go through when you procrastinate, you can think more objectively about what you see. Beyond that advantage, you can use the information from this exercise in other information-gathering exercises in the book. Finally, you'll be using this information in chapter 6 where you create a master plan to curb procrastination.

Key Ideas and Action Plans

Unless you have a photographic memory, it would be difficult to remember all the procrastination awareness and action exercises in this workbook. A highlighter will help you remember what you wish to recall and what makes the most sense for you to do. However, writing down key ideas and action steps gives you something to think about and a prescription to act upon.

Each chapter will have a section at the end for you to write what is important for you to remember (key ideas) and steps to follow (action plan). Use this section to create a coping frame of reference. This method will give you an opportunity to reinforce ideas you find important, as well as to customize design plans to pursue. For example, one key idea is that procrastination is an equal opportunity process that can impact people in any walk of life, in any phase of their life, and in any zone of their life. As for action planning, you can use workbook suggestions as well as create your own strategies. A self-initiated plan, for example, may involve taking an inventory of the ways you procrastinate, ranking them, and identifying the first step to start to effectively master your top procrastination challenge.

To start to implement this key-idea and action-plan approach, think about an area where you procrastinate and where the ideas in this chapter apply. List three ideas from this chapter that you believe make the most sense to you in your quest to deal with procrastination. Then write out three action steps that you can take to make progress. Let's start now:

Key Ideas

1. _____

_____

2. _____

_____

3. _____

_____

Action Plan

1. _____

_____

2. _____

_____

3. _____

_____

This key-idea and action-plan approach has an added benefit. When you're stressed out and caught up in the negative feelings that prompt you to procrastinate, you may not be able to easily remember the helpful ideas and actions to take to help you out of the procrastination pattern. When you can quickly refer to ideas and an action plan you have already found helpful, that you have tested, and that you know you can apply to defeat procrastination, you won't have to rely on your memory to get you going. Through following this approach, you interact with the book's materials and involve yourself in self-regulated learning where you take responsibility for your learning and progress. The more you take control of your procrastination, the stronger your conviction will be that you have the power to overcome the p-factor.

Postscript

Most people who procrastinate are sensitive to being blamed—otherwise they wouldn't invent excuses to deflect or exonerate themselves from blame following a costly delay. Blame is sadly a frequent part of a procrastination process. I've heard many people call themselves stupid for procrastinating, especially when they know they could have ably done what they put off. Some feel humiliated when it becomes clear that they create needless complications for themselves and others. Although it seems simple to avoid the procrastination consequences through acting, it is as though their minds turn off and their impulses take charge. In this regard, it makes no sense to blame yourself for a problem habit. It makes more sense to recognize that habits are ordinarily not intentionally developed, take time to develop, and take time to reverse. Additionally, when you consider that trying to avoid blame all too often results in even longer delays, it just makes practical sense to give yourself a break and begin to confront the process behind the problem.

In the following chapter, we'll explore the benefits of developing a nonblaming perspective. With this nonblaming view in mind, we'll finish the chapter with a Procrastination Inventory that you can use to help yourself catalog factors that merit a close (but nonblaming) review.

CHAPTER 2

Procrastination and Blame

Comedians are great at making a spoof out of procrastination. Have you heard the story of the twenty-three-year-old man who said he wanted to be the oldest person to walk from New York City to Los Angeles? Since he made that declaration, he didn't have to do anything but wait. Some people who know I write procrastination books tell me that they'll buy the book—someday. There are procrastinators' clubs where the self-anointed spokesperson quips that the club hasn't gotten around to electing its officers because no one has gotten around to setting up the election.

Although anybody can make light of procrastination, trivializing the problem provides relief without a solution. Cutting through the procrastination barriers in your life, on the other hand, involves contending with negative processes. I admit that this can be unpleasant, but it's often necessary. On the plus side, your improvement can seem to progress exponentially as you simultaneously build your positive resources to replace the negative. This is a rewarding part of this adventure.

Blame is, perhaps, one of the more significant negative factors you'll have to contend with. In this chapter we'll look at the role blame plays in procrastination and how to stay out of the blame trap. Following that, you'll have an opportunity to complete a procrastination survey. Through this survey, you will identify changeable beliefs that contribute to p-factor patterns. By maintaining a nonblaming view toward your response to the survey items, you can target areas for positive change with the intent of improving your situation.

The Three "E" Factors in Blame

Blame is society's way of assigning consequences. You dent a neighbor's fender, and you're at fault. Your insurance company pays. In this situation, blame is a mechanical process to correct a negative event.

You are likely to operate effectively in most of what you do. But like all fallible humans, you are bound to err. You forget what you went to another room in your home to get. You delayed too long to send a proposal to a good business contact before the person retired. When you use error as a stimulus to correct the situation that led to the mistake, responding affirmatively to reduce your mistakes provides opportunities to build on your positive capabilities.

But we can go overboard on blame and are more likely to do so when living in a "blame culture." Living in such a culture where, like the air, blame is everywhere, you may find yourself structuring part of what you do around avoiding and defending against social and personal forms of blame. In such cultures, we spend too much time blaming ourselves, blaming others, and defending ourselves against blame. That is partially because the propensity to blame is especially acute in westernized cultures where performance is linked to social value—which is linked to personal worth.

Blame cultures are characterized by the three big "E" factors. These are blame excesses, extensions, and exonerations (Knaus 2000). Blame *excesses* include fault-finding, nit-picking, and scolding—blaming for even the smallest fault. The *extensions* go way beyond assigning consequences to causes. We extend blame when we demean, put down, or damn ourselves and others. The idea behind blame *exonerations* is that you hold yourself faultless and shift accountability, such as by saying, "The devil made me do it."

Blame excesses, extensions, and exonerations distract from solving problems, from developing self-improvement skills, and from enjoyment of living. It's hard to feel happy when mired in the negativity of self-blame or when externalizing blame to others. By indulging in blame, we distract ourselves from facing and improving the circumstances that led to the error—inevitably leading to more mistakes and more blame. But blame excesses, extensions, and exonerations are common by-products of living in a blame culture. In theory, the less you blame yourself, the more likely you are to assume responsibility to act upon what is important and positive for you to do.

As you might surmise, blame and procrastination intertwine. Members of the procrastination group prefer to project a favorable public impression. Thus, people will frequently tell themselves one thing to justify procrastinating, such as "later is better," while telling others something entirely different, like the promised materials got blown away by an unexpected gust of wind. The former is self-deception, the latter is an exoneration.

Rather than accept personal responsibility, we are generally more inclined to explain our negative performances based on external conditions. A poor grade in school, for example, is the result of having a "tough teacher." However, if you are in a dysphoric mood (a down mood or the "blues"), you are more likely to blame yourself. You are also more likely to procrastinate. The press of internal stresses like depression can be quite distracting and can interfere with your ability to operate "normally." In a heightened state of stress, you can miss the obvious.

Shifting the blame inward (self-blame) or outward does little to nothing when it comes to finding ways to solve legitimate problems. Evaluating the procrastination situation, refusing to accept lame excuses for inaction, and then concentrating on productive action, even when you feel like running away, is the type of refocus that is likely to yield both short-term and long-term positive results. For example, in acting effectively, do you need certain information? If so, where can you get it? Do you feel like taking a deep breath before starting? Then take a deep breath—and start.

Laziness and Procrastination

Procrastinate, when used as a transitive verb, means to needlessly postpone, delay, or put off a relevant activity until another day or time. Here we concentrate on the behavior and leave character out of the picture. As an intransitive verb, *procrastinate* is defined as putting off doing something out of habitual carelessness or laziness.

Lazy is a common synonym for *procrastination*. It is often a false conclusion. Let's take a closer look at laziness. *Lazy* implies an unwillingness to use effort or energy, or an apathy for activity. But to what activities does this word apply?

Procrastination is rarely a lazy process. People who procrastinate actively avoid what they fear, avoid doing what they find uncomfortable to do, duck what they feel uncertainty about, tell themselves they don't want to waste their time doing something boring or trivial, and so forth. So, rather than an apathy toward activity, a procrastination habit is typically a highly active process where energy and effort is misdirected toward substitute activities.

Blame labels such as "lazy," "careless," "loafer," or "indolent" are examples of blame-culture thinking. Blame labels rarely result in a change of behavior. What they do is encourage the sort of defensiveness where you try to save face or where you retaliate by blaming your accuser. When you feel defensive, you are likely to use your energy to duck the label rather than fix the problem. We typically do better acting to change behavior than to dwell on labels. But if you are going to blame anything, why not blame the brain?

The Procrastinating Brain

You could make a case for blaming your brain for procrastination. Through the process of developing a procrastination habit (which seems to start early in life), the brain modifies itself to accommodate to procrastination thinking, feeling, and actions. Like anything else, we get better at procrastination through practice. After years of putting off unpleasant, boring, or threatening activities, you can overlearn procrastination skills.

In the context of doing something you view as threatening or onerous, procrastination, like fear, may follow brain circuits where you automatically follow a well-grooved process. This process can kick in when you find yourself in a situation that can evoke discomfort. The relief we feel when putting off something unpleasant rewards avoidance or escape activities. This escape/relief sequence originates in the brain.

As it makes no sense to blame yourself for, say, a fear of heights, it makes no sense to blame yourself for a procrastination habit. Blaming your brain is like blaming your genes for an excessive appetite. If you don't want to be overweight, you'll have to grimly accept that you can't eat excessively and still lose weight.

The ability to reason things out is also part of your brain. To the extent this view has merit, it makes sense to find ways to positively alter brain structure and functioning by learning and practicing skills that substitute for procrastination patterns. Blaming yourself for the way your brain reacts when you are in a procrastination mode doesn't do much good. Talking yourself through the paces of following through promises a better solution.

Your prefrontal cortex (new brain) sits at the front of your brain. It is the seat of reasoning, where you override the brain's defensive system when it sets off false alarms like procrastination to avoid discomfort. So, whatever we might observe in the procrastinating brain, the solutions are likely to remain the same: 1. exposing yourself to the procrastination situation; 2. identifying, clarifying, and challenging procrastination self-talk; 3. focusing on following through until this becomes a practiced habit. Throughout this book, you'll learn many ways, such as the PURRRR system, to use your higher reasoning processes to flesh out this three-phase process.

What follows next is the Procrastination Survey. Please complete it in a nonblame atmosphere. This survey is both a general measure of procrastination as well as a helpful diagnostic tool.

The Procrastination Survey

The Procrastination Survey describes different procrastination patterns and reasons why people procrastinate. This seventy-six item survey is followed by scoring instructions telling you how to use the results. Although this is not a standardized measure, the survey is an informal and fun way to look at procrastination. It does not compare people who identify themselves as procrastinators with those who do not believe they procrastinate very much. Its value is that of a flashlight to brighten areas in which you procrastinate.

You can use the survey as a preview for information that you will read about as you progress through this workbook. It gives you a direction for looking more closely at areas where your score suggests a procrastination hot spot.

Procrastination Survey

Directions: Each of the following statements concerns different aspects of procrastination. The survey questions are presented in both positive and negative directions. Your answer is on a four-point scale where 1 = definitely false, 2 = mostly false, 3 = somewhat true, and 4 = definitely true. Circle the number that best describes where you stand on each item.

	Definitely false for me	Mostly false for me	Some-what true for me	Definitely true for me
1. I put off activities of daily living, such as washing, cleaning, auto maintenance, etc.	1	2	3	4
2. I efficiently fulfill responsibilities.	1	2	3	4
3. When I am unsure of an outcome, I'll put it off.	1	2	3	4
4. I have great ideas and plans that stay on the "drawing board."	1	2	3	4
5. I show up late for appointments.	1	2	3	4

6. I look for guarantees before I act.   1   2   3   4

7. I waste too much time.   1   2   3   4

8. When faced with something unpleasant, I tell myself I'll get to it later.   1   2   3   4

9. I devise credible sounding explanations to excuse my delays.   1   2   3   4

10. I know there are personal changes I need to make.   1   2   3   4

11. I expect more of myself than I deliver.   1   2   3   4

12. I stick to my priorities.   1   2   3   4

13. I'm not adequate enough to perform as I want.   1   2   3   4

14. I let work pile up.   1   2   3   4

15. I meet my objective before the deadline.   1   2   3   4

16. I promise myself I'll finish later, then I break my promise.   1   2   3   4

17. I easily get side-tracked.   1   2   3   4

18. I wait to feel inspired before acting.   1   2   3   4

19. To be worthy, I must meet high standards.   1   2   3   4

20. I often start assignments at the last possible minute.   1   2   3   4

21. I am organized and directed in how I achieve major goals.   1   2   3   4

22. I tell myself I'll begin tomorrow.   1   2   3   4

23. I easily make decisions then stick with them.   1   2   3   4

24. I pay bills on time.   1   2   3   4

25. Even when I procrastinate, I'm very demanding of myself.   1   2   3   4

26. My delays hinder others.   1   2   3   4

27. I can't seem to get to places on time.   1   2   3   4

28. I am ready to kick my procrastination habit.   1   2   3   4

	Definitely false for me	Mostly false for me	Some-what true for me	Definitely true for me
29. I daydream a lot.	1	2	3	4
30. I make great progress, then I slip back.	1	2	3	4
31. When I say I'll do something, I get it done quickly.	1	2	3	4
32. I second-guess myself.	1	2	3	4
33. I am more likely to finish when others depend on me.	1	2	3	4
34. My goals are clear, measurable, and achievable.	1	2	3	4
35. I find ways to extend deadlines.	1	2	3	4
36. My "to-do" list remains undone.	1	2	3	4
37. I'm afraid to make a mistake.	1	2	3	4
38. I feel overwhelmed with too many things to do.	1	2	3	4
39. If it's frustrating, I'll avoid it.	1	2	3	4
40. Time seems to "slip away."	1	2	3	4
41. Procrastination comes easily to me.	1	2	3	4
42. When faced with an unpleasant task, I'll do something else first.	1	2	3	4
43. I have bad habits I should break.	1	2	3	4
44. I weigh more than I should.	1	2	3	4
45. I can't stand feeling hassled.	1	2	3	4
46. I don't exercise enough.	1	2	3	4
47. I make plans for getting things done efficiently.	1	2	3	4
48. I quickly face my personal problems.	1	2	3	4
49. I keep to my schedules and meet my deadlines.	1	2	3	4
50. I'm drifting through life.	1	2	3	4
51. I keep things tidy and in their place.	1	2	3	4
52. It may be important, but if I don't feel like doing it, I'll put it off.	1	2	3	4

53. Pushy people deserve to wait.	1	2	3	4
54. I defer making decisions.	1	2	3	4
55. I have the ability to stop procrastinating.	1	2	3	4
56. I procrastinate without forethought.	1	2	3	4
57. I get back at people by delaying them.	1	2	3	4
58. I feel overly stressed.	1	2	3	4
59. When it comes to procrastination, I feel like I am on a yo-yo.	1	2	3	4
60. I worry about what others think.	1	2	3	4
61. I wait until the eleventh hour to begin.	1	2	3	4
62. I meet my responsibilities promptly.	1	2	3	4
63. I cram before exams.	1	2	3	4
64. I'm stressed by too much information to assimilate.	1	2	3	4
65. I'm optimistic about my prospects for beating procrastination.	1	2	3	4
66. I hesitate in making decisions.	1	2	3	4
67. I inconvenience others when I delay.	1	2	3	4
68. I can't seem to get things done on time.	1	2	3	4
69. People expect more from me than I can deliver.	1	2	3	4
70. I think my future looks bright.	1	2	3	4
71. I fear failure.	1	2	3	4
72. People will accommodate me when I turn things in late.	1	2	3	4
73. My moods govern what I do.	1	2	3	4
74. I have trouble making up my mind.	1	2	3	4
75. I worry about what can go wrong.	1	2	3	4
76. I fall short of my standards.	1	2	3	4

Interpretation

This survey taps common procrastination patterns, such as deadline procrastination, and common catalysts, such as self-doubts, that I'll explain throughout this workbook.

The scores on this survey are like golf scores. The higher scores show a potential handicap condition. Where you scored 3 or 4 on the survey, this is a potential procrastination hot spot.

In the "Questions" column, you'll find the question numbers for each hot-spot pattern. If, for example, you scored 4 on 36, you would want to look into behavioral procrastination. The numbers under "Chapter or Page Numbers" are for pages or chapters that specifically relate to the hot spot questions.

	Questions	Chapter or Page Numbers
Procrastination Patterns		
Behavioral Procrastination	4, 36	p. 36, p. 37
Deadline Procrastination	15, 24	p. 2, p. 30
Decision-Making Procrastination	32, 41, 54, 74	Chapter 11
Fallback Pattern	30, 59	p. 37, p. 38
Habitual Procrastination	40, 49	Chapter 10
Health Procrastination	43, 46, 49, 58	Chapter 13
Hindrance Procrastination	53, 57	p. 40, p. 41
Lateness Procrastination	5, 27	p. 38, p. 39, p. 40
Maintenance Procrastination	1, 14	p. 1
Procrastination and Organization	21, 34, 47, 51	Chapter 6, Chapter 14
Personal Procrastination	10, 43, 48, 50	p. 31, p. 32, p. 33
Promissory-Note Procrastination	16, 31	p. 35, p. 36
Social Procrastination	26, 33, 67, 72	p. 29, p. 30, p. 31
General Procrastination	2, 7, 11, 12, 20, 35, 52, 60, 68	p. 41, p. 42, p. 43
Procrastination Catalysts		
Discomfort Dodging	38, 39, 42, 45	p. 45–48, p. 54, p. 102–103
Fear of Failure	6, 37, 69, 71	p. 50, p. 51
Mood	33, 73	p. 8, p. 9, p. 11, p. 33, p. 34, p. 37, p. 48
Perfectionism	11, 19, 25, 76	p. 50–52, p. 124

Survey questions can overlap. For instance, diversions and discomfort avoidance questions sometimes intertwine. It is useful to recognize that procrastination involves a complex interlacing of multiple conditions.

After you've worked on overcoming procrastination for, say, twelve weeks, retake and rescore the survey. This can help you measure where you're making progress and where you have progress to make.

> **Understanding faults brings tolerance and change opportunities.**

Key Ideas and Action Plans

When you look at procrastination, you are looking at a largely negative process with a potentially boondoggling effect on your life. Therefore, it's useful to maintain this perspective: You can reasonably take responsibility for the procrastination process you follow, and, at the same time, keep blame excesses, extensions, and exonerations out of the picture. You'll likely have more energy to direct toward managing procrastination when you are not so distracted by blame.

What key ideas from this chapter can you use to further your plan to decrease procrastination? Write them down. Then write down the actions you can and will take to support a "do it now" initiative.

Key Ideas

1. _____

_____

2. _____

_____

3. _____

_____

Action Plan

1. _____

   _____

2. _____

   _____

3. _____

   _____

Postscript

Procrastination does not follow a neat, clear, design. The process has many subtleties. For instance, although there are numerous individual exceptions, frequent procrastinators tend to use passive expressions to describe their delays such as "I wasn't able to get it." Making yourself directly accountable, while thinking and speaking in an active manner, may support directed acts of responsibility. When your worries cower behind mental walls, they draw energy and time from other matters.

Procrastination has more obvious patterns. Although in a dynamic world with changing situations, perceptions, and perspectives you can expect a variety of procrastination experiences, there is also constancy. Within this constancy, you will find recognizable procrastination forms and styles. The more you know about how these patterns work, the quicker you can recognize and dispense with them. In the following chapter, we'll look at two general forms of procrastination and seven subpatterns.

CHAPTER 3

Procrastination Patterns

You walk into a grocery store and then on to the cereal aisle where you see many different brands. Just as the cereal aisle at your local supermarket has many brands, procrastination presents many varieties. We give descriptive labels to cereal boxes. We can do the same for procrastination.

Labeling can help simplify your understandings of procrastination. But remember, you are not the label. In the procrastination aisle, the label describes a process that occurs within a much broader context labeled "your life."

In this chapter we'll look at two general procrastination patterns and seven related procrastination styles. Naming and describing them can help you understand how they work and how to target ways to change them.

Social Procrastination

When you accept a social responsibility and then procrastinate, you're socially procrastinating. For example, you fear saying no when it comes to doing an acquaintance a favor. You realize that this obligation is discretionary. You really don't want to do the favor. But with a reluctant smile, you agree. Then you don't follow through. Does this sound familiar? If so, welcome to the club—the social procrastinator's club.

Social procrastination, as the label implies, involves delays with social implications. In the world of social procrastination, some delays are impersonal. You prepare your taxes at the eleventh hour, pay credit-card bills late, turn in overdue library books, or delay paying traffic fines. Some members of this *impersonal procrastination* group resent deadlines yet don't like the consequences of delay. So they play out an endless tug-of-war between punctuality and postponement.

Some social procrastination directly impacts our personal relationships. You are likely to get chided if you go along for a free ride on a group project. Social procrastination also comes into play when you believe that the results of your effort won't favorably compare with the work of others. When you procrastinate on group projects to avoid the specter of an unfavorable comparison, you can disadvantage others along with yourself. If you habitually show up late for lunch with friends, you might get the "cold shoulder." Conscientiously meeting your social responsibilities will keep many social hassles off your back.

Deadlines and Due Dates

We all have due dates, more due dates, and still more due dates. You have due dates for paying bills, dates to sign up for selective services, or dates to buy birthday gifts. Some deadlines are absolute. You show up late at the airport, you'll likely miss your flight. Some dates are variable. You ask for an extension to buy extra time to return a library book. We can still procrastinate in the absence of a deadline. Let's say that you know you are in poor shape. Exercise would definitely boost your fitness. When you put this off, you pay a probable cost in appearance, health, and energy.

For those who watch the calendar and clock, due dates are without end. For some, meeting due dates and deadlines is a form of duty whereby they trade off what "society" wants in order to gain advantages in other ways and to avoid the negative consequences of not meeting them. Others view deadlines as demons of duty, and resist every demon that appears on a schedule. Others, like time vagabonds, meander through life, losing track of the clock. When the bells chime, they rush to catch up. In this sense, procrastination is associated with delaying until you bump up against a deadline, finish "under the wire," or miss the date.

It's no mystery why we have deadlines. The Internal Revenue Service compels you to file your taxes by April 15 or file for an extension. Professors have due dates for papers so that they can plan time for reading, reviewing, commenting, and grading. Your community has dates for paying property taxes to have predictable income to pay for staff and services. Organizations that lend money impose a payment schedule so that they can plan and operate. The lenders give you what you want and in exchange, you agree to make payments on a schedule that lets them control the finances of their operation. These external deadlines can stir feelings of resistance. Nevertheless, they are typically effective. Otherwise society would stop using them.

Acting to meet reasonable deadlines, even for externally imposed responsibilities, is a sign of maturity. You show that you are in charge of yourself by sighting past the imposition and going for the benefit of avoiding a big longer-term hassle. In the world of procrastination, following through on these obligatory deadlines is easier said than done.

If you find yourself in this social procrastination trap, you can use the following exercise to put your most significant social procrastination pattern into focus.

How Do You Socially Procrastinate?

1. What is your most pressing social procrastination challenge? (Consider improving your personal communications, fully participating in group endeavors, and paying bills on time.)

_____

_____

2. What do you typically do to avoid the challenge?

_____

_____

3. What do you tell yourself to justify the delay?

_____

_____

4. What actions will you take to follow through to meet the challenge?

_____

_____

Through this exercise you organized information about your primary social procrastination challenge and defined a direction for positive change. The act of citing a procrastination process in writing opens opportunities for evaluating and changing what you see.

Personal Procrastination

Personal procrastination occurs when you routinely put off self-improvement activities that can lead to better physical and psychological health and other personal advantages such as educating yourself, finding a suitable mate, or building a sound career. In the world of personal procrastination, you may delay telling significant people you care about them, avoid taking a risk you've dreamed of taking, or continue to smoke when it's wise to quit. You may not send your job resume out on time and lose an opportunity for a great job. You've also entered the world of personal procrastination when you put off learning to act assertively, saying no when you mean to say no, or where you habitually miss opportunities because you are afraid you will do poorly. Although these personal delays rarely have a fixed deadline, extending them can be seriously handicapping.

People in a personal procrastination pattern often give themselves flimsy excuses to explain their delays: "I am only hurting myself," "There is no rush," "I'll get to it soon." But what does it say about your sense of responsibility to yourself when you decide to delay on important personal-development matters? How is this to be explained?

Unless you directly cope with a personal-development challenge, it's likely to continue. Avoiding looking closely at yourself and your life so that you can make positive changes is generally known as "resistance to change" or "emotional resistance." These labels describe a state where you retreat instead of facing personally uncomfortable or painful challenges. You can also think of it as a special form of procrastination.

By defining and overcoming resistance to change as a series of steps to stop procrastinating, you position yourself to break emotional resistance by taking counter-procrastination actions. Dealing with procrastination in that special personal-development area, you take an important step in progressively mastering personal procrastination by meeting reasonable self-development challenges.

Although effectively coping with procrastination on such things as personal fears certainly won't automatically make the fear disappear, the steps you take to cut through the procrastination barriers that sidetrack you from facing the fear bring you closer to the goal of vanquishing the fear. Some of what you learn about curbing procrastination can apply to overcoming the fear. In later chapters you'll learn more about how to deal with feelings of resistance and avoidance.

You can start personal-development actions anytime. But the challenge is to start sooner rather than later. As an incentive, begin by listing the consequences for personal procrastination delays. For example, do you limit yourself in your abilities to progress? Do you continue with emotional problems because you fear to face them? Then, consider what you gain by facing personal procrastination (self-development) challenges. Are you likely to feel more in charge of your life? Are you likely to gain benefits and advantages? Use the following exercise to put this process into focus.

How Do You Personally Procrastinate?

1. What is your most pressing personal procrastination challenge?

_____

_____

2. What do you typically do to avoid the challenge?

_____

_____

3. What do you tell yourself to justify the delay?

_____

_____

4. What actions will you take to follow through to meet the challenge?

_____

_____

By addressing personal procrastination challenges you cut through resistance to change. You gain advantages through your positive efforts. Can you think of two better reasons to develop your self?

The Social-Personal Connection

Personal procrastination can also negatively affect other people. The person who avoids obtaining needed education for advancement may be penalized by a lower income. The individual's family may have economic limitations as a result. In a more abstract sense, society is deprived of a potential talent. The academic procrastinator who asks the professor for an extension is both self-handicapping and inconveniencing the professor, who may take a dim view on procrastination. You fear criticism for your part of a group project and delay turning in the work. As you put off dealing with a personal fear of criticism, this inconveniences the group.

It rarely does much good to "blame-label" yourself about these social and personal procrastination situations, or guiltily down yourself for what you think you *should* have done. That lamenting is an additional distraction.

Regret, feeling sorry, or feeling disappointed over procrastination is not encumbered with blame labeling or unhealthy guilt. At the level of regret, we are more likely to turn our efforts toward making amends and to correct the problem we created. In this spirit, the roman emperor, Marcus Aurelius (161–180 A.D.), acknowledged that your past is gone and future is uncertain. Although you have no control over the past, you do have control over what you do next—such as avoiding needlessly putting yourself into positions of regret.

Procrastination Styles

Some forms of social or personal procrastination have distinctive features. When you know these features, you can more quickly get to the heart of a procrastination challenge. We'll look at mild-impact procrastination, promissory-note procrastination, behavior procrastination, the fallback pattern, lateness procrastination, hindrance procrastination, and a general procrastination habit. When you read chapter 6 you'll find a comprehensive program for framing and resolving key procrastination challenges where you can further the use of this information to eliminate the p-factor from your life.

Mild-Impact Procrastination

In mild-impact procrastination, important but lower-priority actions get put off. These activities appear to have flexible deadlines where you feel confident that you can stretch the time a bit to do them. In mild-impact procrastination patterns, seemingly small matters can rise to a predicament or crisis. You don't bother to get the skip in your automobile engine checked because you don't feel in the mood. You give yourself the excuse that you have more important things to do. You take a calculated risk that the vehicle won't break down. After weeks of delay, the odds finally go against you. A smiling tow-truck operator holds out a hand for a check before taking your car to a garage.

You tell yourself that you do not want to expend the time and energy to deal with the "little things" that can always be done later. You can always clean the closet, make that phone call, have the car serviced, or clip the hedges later. Still, small matters can accumulate. You can live with the clutter. But what's the point of that?

In the world of mild-impact procrastination, low priorities can eventually rise to high-priority status to compete with normal daily priorities and challenges. Your closets, drawers, garage, and basement fill with clutter, and you feel a nagging sense of frustration when you think about the random collection of junk you've kept. When mild-impact procrastination spreads, people often believe their lives are disorderly and stressful.

Mild-impact procrastination can be stirred by a slightly negative mood where you tell yourself "I don't want to be bothered by this right now." So you lag in keeping up with the details in your life while you await a better frame of mind. The rail in the fence stays on the ground. Weeds start to grow in your flower bed. The mail piles up. Your floor starts to look like a refuse dump. Over time you feel in a malaise. This feeling feeds on itself to the point where a once slightly negative mood generalizes to a pervasive sense of uneasiness. Then, as you view the accumulations of small matters left undone, you might feel overwhelmed thinking that somehow you have to do them all at once, or not at all. Alas, there is no time to do it all now, and so you lag again until you finally feel disgusted and push yourself to sweep away the details by tackling them. However, this press is no fun. When you are done, the thought of doing boring things again adds to your sense of inertia against following through. This is when the pattern can spread into many phases of your life, even to what you normally find fun to do.

To nip this mild-impact procrastination process in the bud, some make up cross-off sheets where they list activities, give each a due date, then check them off as they are done. This approach allows you to see the progress you've made. For routine activities that activities that you regularly delay, photocopy the cross-out sheet and use it many times. Adding several blank lines gives you the opportunity to make adjustments.

As you cross off the activities, you know that you have accomplished two results: You've curbed the procrastination habit and dealt with the activity without undue delay. Once you feel in charge of the small delays in your life, you will have made a major change.

Use the following informational exercise to structure a change in this mild-impact pattern.

Mild-Impact Procrastination and You

1. What is your most pressing mild-impact procrastination challenge?

_____

_____

2. What do you typically do to avoid the challenge?

_____

_____

3. What do you tell yourself to justify the delay?

_____

_____

4. What actions will you take to follow through to meet the challenge?

_____

_____

Action to effectively deal with mild-impact procrastination can free your mind to concentrate on more important matters, such as your personal development.

> Mild-impact procrastination can spread like a fungus.
> Vigilance is important to keep this process in check.

Promissory-Note Procrastination

How often have you made a New Year's resolution only to give it up within hours or days? This is a most common result of a promise to do better when you don't have either a strong commitment or plan to carry through. But this is typically a once-a-year event. The promises you make to yourself then break during the remainder of the year are useful to examine to see if they are worthy of addressing. This evaluation involves why you made them in the first place and why you broke them.

When you make a promise to yourself then don't keep it, you may have good reasons. The need for an action is no longer there. You've learned something to make the matter legitimately less pressing. New goals come into play that supersede the promised goal. But some promises, such as controlling your eating habits, making new friends, getting involved in a community activity, or fulfilling important interests can have strong, ongoing merit. If you don't fulfill your promises to your self in areas where it really matters, you've entered the promissory-note procrastination trap.

In promissory-note procrastination, you have a vision or a wish but not a reasoned plan. Part of this long-term planning involves deciding the *hows, whys, whens,* and *wheres* of bringing about the results that you seek. It involves implementing initiatives by taking the often small steps that lead to your goal.

If you want to keep important promises that you make to yourself, make only those promises that you intend to keep. When you decide to accept a self-promise, you enter the realm of a free choice. Knowing that you could have chosen something else, you can confidently make a good-will effort to actualize your choice. If your prime promises are worth the effort to do, start here to follow through.

Promissory-Note Procrastination and You

1. What is your most pressing promissory-note procrastination challenge?

_____

_____

2. What do you typically do to avoid the challenge?

_____

_____

3. What do you tell yourself to justify the delay?

_____

_____

4. What actions will you take to follow through to meet the challenge?

_____

_____

When you make a promise to yourself, it is worth noting whether the change you contemplate is sufficiently meaningful to warrant the time and effort to bring it about. A promise worth making is worth keeping, even when it is to yourself.

Behavioral Procrastination

In promissory-note procrastination, you have a wish without a plan. In behavioral procrastination, you have both a wish and a plan, but the breakdown still happens when you try to get started.

Although behavioral procrastinators can have outstanding visions, make great plans, and even get organized, they normally don't follow through. The effect is like starting a foot race running fast, then sitting down just before the finish line as you watch others run past you to get the prize. Understandably, behavioral procrastination befuddles many who start strong then fade at the finish.

The behavioral procrastination process appears in different disguises. Some think about starting their own business, study how to go about succeeding in business, create elaborate business plans, and then don't go beyond the plan. Others accumulate projects that remain unfinished. For example, you get all excited about planting for the spring, visit your local nursery to gather gardening materials and bulbs for planting, but you keep putting off actually getting out and preparing the soil. Or you research a promising new career, identify the right employers, create a great resume, practice interviewing, and do everything thoroughly—up to the point of applying for the job you want.

The behavioral procrastinator gets to the brink of execution then waits for inspiration to hit. Planning is the fun part. Execution, on the other hand, requires a set of skills the consummate planner finds frustrating to do. If you get into the behavioral procrastination trap, plan to test each phase of what you designed to do. It is here where you discover adjustments that can help improve the overall plan.

Behavioral procrastination is like getting to the pot of gold then letting someone else take it away. Use the following exercise to go for the gold by following through with the plan.

Behavioral Procrastination and You

1. What is your most pressing behavioral procrastination challenge?

_____

_____

2. What do you typically do to avoid the challenge?

_____

_____

3. What do you tell yourself to justify the delay?

_____

_____

4. What actions will you take to follow through to meet the challenge?

_____

_____

Following through on meaningful projects substitutes a gain for a loss. However, if you start with zero, execute the plan, and end with zero, you've neither gained nor lost advantage. You will have learned more about what works and what doesn't. By following through with your plans, the odds favor that you can build a list of ways to advantage yourself.

The Fallback Pattern

Some people follow a circular procrastination-action-procrastination-action pattern. They habitually fall behind, panic, and go into a flurry of activity to catch up. Then, with a sense of overconfidence that they have beaten the pattern, they soon "slip" and fall behind again. People who fall into these circular procrastination patterns initially make gains, then relapse to the patterns they thought they escaped. Fallback patterns can be as gradual as they are dramatic. Here we find the person who loses fifty pounds then gains seventy back within the next year. The fallback pattern also appears in other ways. You exercise for a time, then stop, then start again. Have you ever tried to cut back on your credit-card debt, succeeded, then gotten back into the same financial fix that you recently vacated? Perhaps the most common fallback pattern is after following productive actions, you glide into a state of lethargy, then back to purposeful action, then back to lethargy. For a time, the discipline was there—then lost. What happened?

Like mild-impact procrastination, the fallback pattern can be mood related. When you feel in a positive mood, you're more likely to be proactive. Then you experience a negative mood, and you fall back if the mood feels drawn out. The fallback pattern can also show overconfidence. Suppose you make a diligent effort to be punctual, to throw off distracting details as they arise, and follow through on personal challenges. After a while, you think that this consistency is automatic and will continue without the same special effort you made when you operated effectively. But action is more often mechanical than automatic. Fallback starts when effort declines.

This start-stop, start-again, stop-again procrastination pattern is an example of conscientiousness. (Buying this workbook also is an act of conscientiousness.) You _want_ to do better and you keep trying. If you see yourself in the fallback pattern, this is evidence that you want to change and have made many conscientious efforts to do so. Perhaps through using critical ideas that you learn here, you can teach yourself to operate with greater consistency.

Each fallback procrastination form can involve different change strategies. If the fallback pattern coincides with a recurrent negative mood, then deal with curbing the procrastination that delays your dealing with the mood. If you find yourself in a "flurry of activities" fallback phase where you rush to beat the clock, this also suggests a desire to act conscientiously and responsibly. Part of dealing with this type of pattern involves accepting that consistency is a way to move away from crisis management to self-discipline.

Fallback patterns lead to collections of incomplete tasks from the past that can haunt your present and dampen your future. Reversing the process by maintaining consistency can give you a different point of view. Use the following to help yourself to consistently exercise your conscientiousness drives.

Fallback Procrastination and You

1. What is your most pressing fallback procrastination challenge?

_____

_____

2. What do you typically do to avoid the challenge?

_____

_____

3. What do you tell yourself to justify the delay?

_____

_____

4. What actions will you take to follow through to meet the challenge?

_____

_____

By withdrawing from the fallback pattern, you'll sense that you are more truly in charge of what you do. You also will have arrested a pervasive pattern through exercising your conscientiousness drives.

Lateness Procrastination Patterns

Are you one of the millions who show up late for appointments and meetings? Do you leave friends waiting for you to arrive at the movies after the show has begun? Do you arrive at parties as the other guests are leaving? This is the lateness procrastination pattern. Like a chameleon, it changes:

- People caught in this last-minute procrastination pattern often act like their priority was to get "little things" out of the way before they depart. You may wash, shower, fix your hair, or tidy a room at the time you need to leave. You may sip a second cup of coffee rather than get ready. You may make that phone call to a long-winded friend. In these instances, you have lost sight of your priority, which is to get to where you are going on time.

- You make some preparatory efforts to get organized so that you can leave on time. Then you underestimate the time it takes to put on your coat, go to the garage to get the automobile, warm up the car, and so forth. A perpetual optimist, you believe that you'll make all the lights, and traffic will be light. You arrive fifteen minutes late, blaming traffic.

- Some fall into this last-minute pattern when they don't take time to organize themselves. The time comes to depart, and we find such persons rushing about looking for keys, packing, finishing last-minute work, and trying to find a copy of the report they just put down.

- Suppose you hate to wait. You really don't want to get to your destination early because you don't think you will know what to do with yourself during the time between your arrival and the event. So you dilly-dally just long enough to make yourself late, usually so late that you feel embarrassed.

- A lateness procrastination pattern can reflect a *trace procrastination* condition. This is a form of procrastination that once served a purpose. It exists, so to speak, because it *has* existed. You were, say, socially anxious five years ago. Diversionary delays once slowed your appearance at social situations and avoiding these situations provided a temporary relief. But this is no longer an issue. You even look forward to meeting with new people, as well as with old friends. You really do want to get to places on time or before time. You know the benefits and feel good when you reach your destination without rushing in breathlessly. But the lateness habit is now so well practiced that you retrace the old ways even when you want to adopt new ways.

Lateness procrastination is among the most frustrating procrastination styles. If you feel harried by a lateness-procrastination pattern, position yourself to change it. To set the stage for this choice, explore the sequence you follow when you are involved in this pattern. What happens first, second, and third? What is the typical result of the lateness-procrastination habit? What can you do to break the cycle at each of the points in this process? For example, you can choose to ignore last minute tidying until after you return from your destination. You can plan to leave with time to spare so you can get to your destination fifteen minutes early. You may find that ignoring last minute distractions is more an advantage than a disadvantage. This progressive effort keeps you in focus on the priority of getting to places on time. This effort requires concentration, but it pays off in lessening the amount of time you feel frazzled, rushed, and embarrassed by being late again.

An important reward for getting places on time is the control that comes from knowing you no longer fritter away time in busywork, and you can accurately estimate the time it takes to get to different places on time. Use the following exercise to get that reward, starting now.

Lateness Procrastination and You

1. What is your most pressing lateness procrastination challenge?

_____

_____

2. What do you typically do to avoid the challenge?

_____

_____

3. What do you tell yourself to justify the delay?

_____

_____

4. What actions will you take to follow through to meet the challenge?

_____

_____

In lateness-procrastination patterns, you engage in a flurry of busywork activities that probably don't do much to allay tension. The result of these distractions is to produce a feeling of being rushed. Release from this pattern can feel liberating.

Hindrance Procrastination

We're all going to have times when we feel peeved at someone, then delay them. However, this reaction suggests a negative, roundabout way to solve a problem.

In *hindrance procrastination*, you intentionally obstruct others through delays. In a hindrance state of mind, people are inclined to put things off if their delays get back at someone. But when you put off doing something that's also to your benefit because you are trying to hurt someone else, it's like shooting a hole in your boat because someone asked to use it. Diplomatically or assertively addressing the matters that typically lead to hindrance opens opportunities for better communication and sense of control over the situations you encounter where directness pays dividends. However, commanding yourself to do what is in your enlightened self-interest takes a sense of maturity and responsibility that can be easily obscured within a negative, "get even" state of mind.

There will be times when you'll feel like dragging your heels when someone tries to pressure you to do what you would voluntarily have done or speaks down to you as though you were ignorant of what you find obvious. A supervisor nitpicks at your work, speaks in a critical tone, treats you like a child, and tells you to do what you would normally have done without instructions. You note this supervisor does the same with the majority of others except for a few favored employees. Your first impulse is to resist, slow down, and throw stumbling blocks in the supervisor's path. You might first feel a triumphal sense of satisfaction if you operate in this manner. But eventually hindrance reactions lead to tensions, brooding, and conflicts.

I'll admit that dealing with difficult people, especially the controlling and nitpicking kind, is frustrating. It is tempting to hinder them or try to beat them at their own game. However, if you decide that this is not a healthy contest, you can always take the high road and focus on the prime issue, proceeding to move forward. But first you have to see the high road. That is the path you might rationally tell a good friend to take under similar circumstances.

Some hinder others to see what they can get away without doing. If you fall into this version of the trap, you can pay a double price. You can stress yourself, and you risk alienating people who might eventually be in a position to provide a needed favor. Through constructive action you can put a freeze on the social and personal procrastination that spin from this view and end up hurting you.

There is a personal-health side to hindrance-procrastination patterns. Chronic hostility is a documented health risk factor that correlates with coronary heart disease (Todd et al. 1996). By effectively defusing this health-risk hindrance procrastination style, you'll have less to fume about and more of a sense of positive personal control. You are likely to give others less reason to hinder you. This creates more of a win-win condition that will get you further than hindrance ever could. Use the following exercise to start decreasing hindrance procrastination.

Hindrance Procrastination and You

1. What is your most pressing hindrance-procrastination challenge?

_____

_____

2. What do you typically do to avoid the challenge?

_____

_____

3. What do you tell yourself to justify the delay?

_____

_____

4. What actions will you take to follow through to meet the challenge?

_____

_____

When you act to decrease hindrance, you simultaneously act to develop tolerance. Developing tolerance is quite different from acting passively. In tolerance development you act to correct problems, first by putting the situation into perspective and then by acting to address the problems you face. A gradually increasing sense of tolerance can feel like paradise compared to the negative feelings that typically precede and accompany hindrance urges.

General Procrastination Problem Habits

Procrastination can be a *symptom* of a spectrum of complications including self-doubts and discomfort dodging. It can be a *defense* against a fear of failure or shame. Procrastination also can be a general *problem habit*. Like most problem habits, the process of procrastination thinking, feeling, and acting occurs without much conscious forethought.

At a general habit level, procrastination is the result of a complex interaction of psychological, chemical, and muscular processes. Because of this interacting network, a general procrastination habit can prove challenging to change, especially if you go through the procrastination paces without realizing it.

General procrastination habits are invasive in the sense that you feel habitually inclined to put off what you know you can easily do. That is because this habit follows well-worn pathways, is well-practiced, and operates like a radio wave. You can't see it, but the elements are there to hear if you have the right receiver operating.

Although you can have exceptional potential for breaking negative habit patterns, to make this talent useful, you have to exercise it. Breaking a problem procrastination habit involves 1. directly and honestly facing what you do when you procrastinate, 2. committing yourself to accept any discomfort that spikes when you act to curb the process, and 3. accepting that you'd best reprogram yourself to think more clearly and act more effectively. This is not so daunting as it can appear. For example, you've taken a real step in breaking a procrastination habit pattern when you persistently act to change one part of the pattern. Part of this involves changing your perspective on your procrastination catalysts. For example, at the initial stages of procrastination you can view discomfort about doing a task as all the more reason to *do it now*.

It takes a deliberate effort to recognize and curb any aspect of a general procrastination pattern. An exercise that allows you to trace back each step of the pattern can give you a different perspective on understanding and dismantling this process. In this exercise, you go from the endpoint to the beginning, starting with 5 and ending with 1.

Trace Back the Pattern

5. At what point do you act to clear up a long-delayed commitment? (When time is running out?)

4. At what point do you decide to act? (When it is clear that you can no longer tolerate the consequences of delay?)

3. How do you lull yourself into complacency so that you further delay? (Do you tell yourself you have plenty of time?)

2. What do you first tell yourself to start delaying? (Do you tell yourself you are too tired, not ready, or the activity is a waste of time?)

1. What happens when you are first aware of an urge to procrastinate? (Do you view the activity as tedious, boring, or threatening?)

By focusing on the point of decision to act and then the actions themselves, you might come to break the habit. You can use the initial discomfort as a catalyst to leapfrog to the decision to act and to the action stage. Skipping the preliminary stages of procrastination and getting to the action is a mental leap, but one that you can profitably practice.

By putting the procrastination process in reverse, you can accomplish the following: 1. you analyze the process in a different way; 2. you get a different angle on what is happening; 3. you can see that you actually got done what you've put off doing; 4. you identified the point of decision where you judged that the time had come to act. 5. you recognize there is a lot of busywork and distractions that get in the way and further the delay.

When you practice follow-through actions, you exercise control over this habit process. As a by-product, you are better able to develop your positive competencies. Use the following to start this process:

Your General Procrastination Habit

1. What is your most pressing general procrastination habit challenge?

_____

_____

2. What do you typically do to avoid the challenge?

_____

_____

3. What do you tell yourself to justify continuing the habit?

_____

_____

4. What actions will you take to break the habit?

_____

_____

You can force yourself to retreat from a generalized procrastination pattern by taking steps to establish and practice a *do it now* habit. You may have to continue this practice over a lifetime so that the *do it now* habit stays strongly rooted enough to ably override the automatic procrastination habit process. But through coping with general procrastination, the payoff repeatedly occurs as you strengthen your self-regulation abilities to boost your sense of competency. Effectively meeting the general procrastination challenge is an important way to boost your sense of personal efficacy.

Key Ideas and Action Plans

The two procrastination styles and seven procrastination patterns overlap, interlace, and can sometimes feel like they are different aspects of a single procrastination process. In one sense, that's positive. By learning to deal with one form of procrastination, you can develop skills to deal with the others.

By writing out the procrastination processes and creating an action plan, you act to slow the procrastination process and scrutinize what you do. What are the key ideas from this chapter that you believe you can use to further your plan to decrease procrastination? Write them down. Then write down the actions you can and will take to support a *do it now* outcome.

Key Ideas

1. _____

_____

2. _____

_____

3. _____

_____

Action Plan

1. _____

_____

2. _____

_____

3. _____

_____

Postscript

It's often said that the simplest explanations are more often the right ones. If we follow these approaches, we test the simple ideas before seeking more complicated explanations. For example, you note that your neighbor fenced her vegetable garden to keep wild rabbits out. If you thought this was proof that she was the leader of a world-wide conspiracy to starve these little furry critters, that would be a bit far-fetched. The simplest explanation is that your neighbor wants to protect her vegetable garden, and that's most likely all there is to it.

The simplest definition for *procrastination* describes a process: We procrastinate when we do something else that is less important. The simple solution is first to do what you are tempted to delay. But since we rarely can oppose an oppressive procrastination habit pattern with a simple declaration, you are wise to go to the next simplest level, which we'll take up next when we look into procrastination complications.

CHAPTER 4

Procrastination Complications

Procrastination can represent many complicating conditions. For example, people who persistently procrastinate can be driven by factors such as indecisiveness, risk aversion, low frustration tolerance, rebellion, a fear of failure, indifference, boredom with the task, and/or impulse-control problems. In this chapter we'll look at four common underlying conditions that I find associated with procrastination: low frustration tolerance and discomfort dodging, self-doubts, contingency worth, and perfectionism. These conditions often overlap so it is sometimes challenging to separate one from the other. A core problem-solving approach involves addressing them when they help mechanize a procrastination habit.

Whatever the causes of procrastination, the solution is to switch from procrastination diversions to *do it now* actions.

Low Frustration Tolerance and Discomfort Dodging

None of us can totally avoid frustration. Many times during the day you'll find yourself hindered or your goals blocked. Your pet peeve list probably includes many frustration producers. You go to the post office, and a long-winded person ties up the clerk while deciding what style of stamp to purchase. You're in a hurry, and a coworker wants to talk your ear off. You call a merchant, and stay on hold long enough to feel a slow burn.

While frustration is normal and even desirable in many situations, low frustration tolerance reflects a rise in the intensity of frustration when you add negative thinking to an already frustrating situation. For example, while waiting in line at the post office, you start to think that you *can't stand* waiting any longer. You start tapping your fingers, your heart rate goes up—you've entered the low-frustration-tolerance zone.

Procrastination can have many catalysts, but low frustration tolerance is probably the most common. In this frame of mind, the procrastination process engages when you think the task before you is intolerable. You believe that you simply won't be able to handle the frustration that the task will bring, and you sidetrack yourself. You can talk yourself into a scrambling retreat for bogus low frustration tolerance reasons: "It's too hard," "I don't know where to begin," "I can't do this now," "Oh no! This is too much (too tough, too unpleasant, too bothersome)."

Low frustration tolerance is a common trigger for discomfort dodging: 1. you feel uncomfortable as you anticipate facing an unwanted situation; 2. you are sensitive to signals of discomfort, over-focus on them, and distract yourself from the priority activity; 3. you focus attention on your tension, and the *attention* you pay to the *tension* magnifies your feelings of stress, resulting in your feeling less and less capable of concentrating and proceeding.

When you focus on and magnify the discomfort you feel, this lowers your frustration tolerance, and increases a tendency to procrastinate in an effort to avoid what you perceive as horribly difficult. This is a prime reason why low frustration tolerance and frustration avoidance are at the core of much human misery and distress.

With time and practice, the thought of doing something useful but unpleasant can spark a complex process of retreat that often includes promises to do better later accompanied by substitute activities that typically give an immediate sense of relief (like putting your bills aside for another day and turning on the TV). Like apparitional figures, these discomfort-dodging directions dance through our mind and beat the drum for a retreat that keeps us on the brink of defeat.

Persistent low frustration tolerance leads to frustration tolerance disturbances. This is a consistent state of frustration-based tension where even small challenges feel like huge strains and avoidance begins to seem like the only option. This combination of a low-frustration frame of mind and tension couples with feelings of unhappiness and often triggers negative thoughts about your life.

People with high frustration tolerance are going to experience less stress, accomplish more, and feel better about themselves. Facing up to your frustrations, building tolerance for them, and acting to solve problems associated with these feelings is a prime way to take charge of the way you'd prefer your life to go.

Low Frustration Self-Talk

If you are in a low frustration or frustration disturbance frame of mind, there are no guarantees that you'll feel happy as a result of your proactive efforts. But waiting for a change of mood is sometimes like waiting for a change of menu at a specialty restaurant. If you don't like the menu, try a different place.

A new approach to building frustration tolerance involves facing the frustration through action. This is a positive, affirmative way to directly deal with a hindrance or impediment. Decreasing negative thinking about the impediment can lift your mood and will go a long way toward helping you reach your goal. As a first step, identify and deal with negative low frustration tolerance self-talk.

You can recognize aspects of low frustration tolerance through the words you use to describe experience. When faced with a frustrating task, you might tell yourself, "It's too tough," or "I can't stand doing this," or "It's awful that I have to be inconvenienced this way." These are examples of low-frustration-tolerance self-talk. This type of negative inner dialogue match with frustrated frames of mind and negative moods.

Dealing with Low-Frustration-Tolerance Self-Talk

The words and phrases we use when our tolerance for frustration is lost exaggerate and dramatize the negativity of activities. By magnifying and dramatizing the negatives in a priority activity, you are more likely to procrastinate. You also are likely to feel anxious. To shift from distressful ways of thinking to a positive self-regulated approach, think out the meaning of what you tell yourself when you ready yourself to procrastinate. For example, what makes doing the task too tough for you? Is the *too tough* idea an automatic thought? What part of the activity is manageable? If you have a place to start, then what does this say about the theory that the task's too tough?

Regarding the "I can't stand it" idea, what is the *it* that you think you can't stand? Is the *it* discomfort? What can you do about the *it*?

By identifying the surplus meaning in a low-frustration-tolerance phrase, you position yourself to cut the surplus meaning out from the activity. If you think that doing something you find necessary but unpleasant is awful, you've added a big surplus meaning. On the other hand, if an activity is unpleasant, accepting the unpleasantness can make the experience feel more tolerable.

When you have a priority activity to do, feel a surge of frustration, and tell yourself "I don't want to," first reflect on what you don't want to do. Then ask yourself, why? For example, "I don't want to do it because, 1. the activity is too uncomfortable, 2. the activity is too difficult, 3. I can't stand doing what I don't like." If you tell yourself that the activity is *too* uncomfortable, then what makes it *too* uncomfortable for you to do? If you can't stand what you don't like, what makes the situation so intolerable? By reflecting on the impact of such low-frustration-tolerance words and phrases, you can discover that you'll still find the task unlikable, but that doesn't make it intolerable.

Switching from low-frustration-tolerance distractions to *do it now* activities involves exposing yourself to discomfort you'd normally avoid by procrastinating. When you don't run from this discomfort, you help yourself build tolerance for it. This discomfort acceptance modifies the meaning of the discomfort, making the feeling useful as an incentive for solving problems. You can further short-circuit the low-frustration-tolerance procrastination process through PURRRR.

1. When you face a pressing and relevant situation where you experience a feeling of resistance to following through, *pause.*

2. Suppress your procrastination *urges* by refusing to act on them.

3. *Reflect* on your thinking, avoidance urges, and what you feel tempted to do to dodge the frustration. Put this process into slow motion by thinking about your thinking or writing it out.

4. In the *reason* phase, separate out and evaluate low-frustration-tolerance self-talk. If you tell yourself you can't do it until you feel more comfortable, ask yourself where that tomorrow view has gotten you in the past. The odds are that this promissory delay is a prelude to another. If you think the task is too uncomfortable, ask yourself what you mean by *too*? It's usually when you make a project into a composite and see it as wholly uncomfortable that you are likely to lose sight of what you can do. Then look at the initial steps you can take that you can do first, or now. There is practically always one aspect to a challenge that you can manage. Through this problem-mapping analysis, you put a very challenging procrastination condition into perspective, and position yourself for action.

5. Following reason, *respond* by taking mapped steps to crack your low-frustration-tolerance barriers. In this process, think the action directions silently to yourself. This helps quell impulses to shift your thoughts elsewhere, such as on reading a novel. Then follow your plan by walking yourself through the paces in the direction of accomplishment. Take the first step. Then talk yourself through the second step. Keep doing this until you build a momentum to get done what you normally would put off because of low-frustration-tolerance self-talk.

6. If you bog down, *revise* your self-directions. Then put your muscles into motion. Actions to break procrastination's inertial barriers move like an arrow toward the center of a target. Not all arrows hit the bull's-eye, but practice and adjustments in technique help shape the results for a higher hit rate. Reasoning and responding include sighting and releasing; *revising* is like the adjustment phase. Here you look at the results of actions to impose reason between procrastination perceptions and reactions. You adjust your aim and method. This shift can involve introducing new techniques such as allowing yourself to experience discomfort as part of the procrastination pause-and-action-suppression phase of this process. If you've overlooked a step, the revision can include adding the missing step.

Self-Doubt Procrastination

People who doubt themselves are primed to second-guess themselves, hesitate, and procrastinate. So you avoid new challenges and opportunities unless success is guaranteed. Since such guarantees are rare, you wait until you can make a sure decision. This indecision translates into delays in executing a productive course of action.

When self-doubts and fear of discomfort interact, the combination prompts a vicious circle of doubt-and-discomfort-dodging procrastination. Left unchecked, doubt-and-discomfort-dodging procrastination can affect your global self-worth. For example, people who suffer from low self-esteem tend to put less time and effort into dealing with their negative moods (Heimpel et al. 2002). Procrastination on disabling negative moods can fuel a sense of helplessness, and more self-doubts.

Members of the self-doubt group have areas in their lives where they make themselves anxious by defining a challenge as unmanageable, too tough, or overwhelming. The talented writer sits before an empty pad of paper, a sharpened pencil sitting nearby. She never gets started because her self-doubts have crowded out her ideas and inspirations.

In a pique of self-doubt, some make half-hearted efforts while thinking they could do better if they tried harder. Other self-doubters go to the other extreme. They drive themselves, fearing that if they let down their guard, they will become lazy and unable to act. Through engaging in pressured efforts, people caught in this cycle typically procrastinate on finding ways to have a relaxed, enjoyable, fulfilling existence.

Habits of self-doubt evoke feelings of insecurity. Such insecurities are often based upon myths, misconception, perfectionist expectations, and other self-defeating beliefs based on faulty assumptions about reality.

Altering a Self-Doubt View

When procrastination is an extension of self-doubt, there are two basic challenges: 1. to develop a fact-based belief system about yourself; 2. to refuse to needlessly delay in order to develop self-regulating skills and a sense of self-efficacy. Both represent reversals of the doubt-procrastination cycle.

Children are generally poor at monitoring their thinking, and many adults are not much better. Yet this is an important place to begin to understand the self-doubting, second-guessing, hesitation part of a procrastination cycle. For example, what do you tell yourself about your ability to withstand discomfort or uncertainty when you procrastinate out of doubt? This type of question can give you an opportunity to examine what you think when you procrastinate due to doubt.

Second-guessing and hesitating is a classic form of indecisiveness leading to procrastination. Often you might want to avoid a mistake or don't want to act without overwhelming confirmation that the choice you make will be safe. So you equivocate, quibble with yourself, and worry about endless possibilities. But some situations are going to be ambiguous until you engage them to gain clarity. Pettifogging them through second-guessing yourself adds another layer of distraction. If you reach a hesitation phase, consider what you can learn if you erred in a decision; what could you gain if your decision translated into action that brought an advantage that you otherwise would not have experienced? If you are 51 percent sure of a direction, you'll likely have to make modifications as you learn the results of your initial actions in that direction. However, 51 percent is a reason to act to test the waters.

Contingent-Worth Procrastination

The clock was developed in the 1300s partially in response to urbanization and the need to measure production against some standard. That gave us a uniform yardstick for assessing how well we use time for productive purposes.

In time-performance-oriented societies, our financial worth and status is often tied to how effectively and profitably we use our time. Unfortunately, people in time/production cultures commonly make magical jumps from the worth of their timed performances to their global self-worth by using what we call contingency-worth standards. One version of the contingency-worth formula is this: Use time wisely and you are worthy; don't use time wisely and you are unworthy. Of course, this is a silly idea. But it has been around for centuries. Maybe the notion has lasted so long because there's a grain of truth it it. After all, if you use time wisely, you are likely to gain advantages. Fritter it away, and there is a price to pay. This doesn't mean that you're worthless if you waste time, but you probably know that it's to your benefit to use time well.

If you use time to perform, and your performance is exceptional, your personal worth index rises. But this outlook is like being on a yo-yo. When you feel up, you worry that your next move will be down. Acting like you believe your human worth depends on how you use time, you practically guarantee that you will experience stress, and this type of stress makes procrastination look like a pleasing alternative.

Striving for excellence can result in big and valuable rewards. Doing the best you can within the time and resources you have available promises greater benefit and advantage than an "I'll get to it later" mentality. Focusing on what you can do rather than worrying about how you are doing is an additional benefit, as you can learn positive things about your attributes when you are engaged in action compared with negative contemplations.

Despite the advantages of doing well, there is a mental twist that can turn this process into a cesspool. The "achievement-equals-worth" belief is a nightmare for millions, especially males who are traditionally taught that they must achieve wealth and power in order to be worthy. This contingency view inspires procrastination among those who don't think they can "measure up. " We see procrastination to avoid failure among those who think that whoever comes in second is the first loser. Predictably, people with a high expectation for success, have a low tolerance for error. This view dovetails with a fear of failure that readily ignites a path to procrastination.

Perfectionist striving to be the best there is or ever was sets unrealistic conditions for worth that quickly connect to distress. This contingency view is risky for those who believe that the "self" is measured by success or failure. What does it mean, then, when you fall beneath standard? You enter the domain of a self-defined failure.

Altering a Contingent-Worth View

Contingency-worth thinking represents extreme ways of thinking. Fortunately, this extreme isn't written in stone. When you accept that personal worth is not dependent upon isolated performances, and that you can likely feel better about yourself and what you are doing without the specter of failure hovering omnipresent, you'll realize that holding yourself to unrealistic standards isn't beneficial.

As an alternative to contingency-worth beliefs, consider this philosophy: 1. strive for excellence by following a *do it now* process; 2. seek balance by allowing yourself ample time for recreation, relaxation, companionship, and "downtime;" 3. take on reasonable challenges that stretch your resources; 4. follow through to experience your most cherished visions and dreams.

You also can look upon what you do as experiments where you try to find out what works and what doesn't. In this way you douse the flames of failure by philosophically eliminating it.

Perfectionism and Procrastination

Perfectionism is as much a primitive form of superstitious thinking as is fearing to cross a black cat's path. These days few think that by avoiding this cat's path you can avoid bad luck. In a perfectionist frame of mind you think you can avoid disaster through perfection.

A common perfectionist belief is that to obtain safety, security, certainty, and human worth you must meet specific standards. With high standards and a sensitivity toward mistakes and errors, members of this group have their defect-detectors on high alert. Living life with defect detectors on high alert orients us toward dwelling on what went wrong, what is currently going wrong, and what can go wrong. In this world of negativity, fear, anxiety, and depression flourish unchecked.

This hypersensitive attitude of mind is an open invitation to procrastination. In a perfectionist mind-set, you are rarely satisfied, typically anxious, and frequently distracted from directly acting. The approach for improvement involves exposing negative demand thinking that detracts from effectiveness. The perfectionist view translates into a narrow definition of self-value where this demand thinking becomes painfully judgmental. Falling short of the mark you set, you might hear yourself thinking in coercive blame cliches such as, "You stupid idiot, you should have known better," or "What's wrong with you? Can't you get anything right?" To avoid feeling stupid, many perfectionists will procrastinate in areas where they feel vulnerable to this inner censure.

Perfectionism involves rigid expectations that lead to a yo-yo cycle of worth where you feel up when you do well and demoralized when you don't. There is no compromise in this philosophical system, such as finding a middle ground where you feel only partially demoralized.

Since perfectionist-driven procrastination often leads to delays, some members of this group occasionally try to make up for lost time. They periodically pressure themselves in uncompromising ways and gain little satisfaction for the sweat of their accomplishment. In their mind, whatever they do is never quite good enough. Other perfectionist procrastinators engage in busywork where they substitute low-priority (and low-risk) activities for the more important tasks of the day.

Perfectionism is rarely so pervasive as to cause you to feel incapacitated 100 percent of the time. Most perfectionists do get things done and are productive to varying degrees. Nevertheless, perfectionists are excessively demanding. They insist, require, and expect compliance to often rigid rules and standards. Some drive and stress themselves to achieve. Others second-guess themselves, hesitate, and procrastinate. Understandably, at either extreme they are going to experience performance anxiety. This is an irrational fear of not living up to what others expect from them and what they expect from themselves.

A procrastination solution for perfectionism is to wait to discover safe and guaranteed solutions prior to meeting challenges. You can see this in people who fear failure and seek certainty to assure security. Without guarantees, they need to play it safe. Here, even making inconsequential decisions is a scary thing. If you fall into this trap, over time you can feel overwhelmed with a full in-basket and with little in the out-basket.

Some fear-of-failure perfectionists believe that other people are superior and that one must be perfect to be simply acceptable. Members of this threat-sensitive group fall into a vicious cycle. They doubt themselves, second-guess themselves, equivocate, hesitate, and put themselves down for many of the things they do or avoid doing. In this case, fear of failure reflects a fear of not being adequate enough and not measuring up. It's all hocus-pocus, but feels very threatening to people with inventive minds who wave a wand and define themselves as potential failures by virtue of often vague standards, unrealistic comparisons with others, and faulty assumptions that negative thinking makes something so.

Some perfectionists conclude that their presence is an offense to others. In such cases, the following phrase can help put this obligatory perfection expectation into a humorous perspective: "Please forgive me for not being what I think you think I ought to be. Forgive me for offending thee by being me."

Altering a Perfectionist View

The perfectionist philosophy is, "I must be what I think I should be, or I'm nothing at all." This one-way thinking sets the stage for tension. If you know the philosophy behind perfectionist thinking, you can counter it with a broader view.

In adopting a more expansive way of thinking, you consider that you have about eighteen thousand characteristics that include attributes that surface depending on a situation and your perception of that situation. You have spatial abilities, verbal abilities, problem-solving abilities, physical skills, creative abilities, organizing abilities—and the list goes on. You have the potential for over five-hundred different types of emotions, including the hard-wired primary type for fear, anger, love, attachment, frustration, sadness, and curiosity and secondary types that include compassion, concern, and hope. You have values, attitudes, and beliefs. You have the potential to modify many of the ways that you think, as well as direct the way you choose to act in changing situations.

By shifting perspective to a pluralistic philosophy, you can feel more confident in that philosophy than with the one-way-street, static, perfectionist philosophy. With a pluralistic view, many things continue to go right even when some feel disappointing. With this pluralistic view, it is easier to adopt another.

In a perfectionist frame of mind, you operate out of a *requiring* philosophy, live by standards that you think are reasonable, but are typically unrealistic. Just like procrastination has an opposite *do it now* view, a requiring philosophy has as its opposite an aspiring philosophy. Here you aspire to do well, prefer to perform effectively, and desire positive results. You don't demand impossible perfection! The aspiring view involves thinking in terms of preferences, wishes, wants, and desires. In this realistic and optimistic mind-set, your thinking is flexible, motivation heightened, and you go after what you desire. In short, you do the best you can under the time and conditions available. This is the *do it now* way.

Members of the aspiring philosophy group typically feel relaxed as they reflectively think things through before committing themselves to action. They measure the likelihood of achieving their dreams and realize that each dream has a start and markers along the way. When they strive for excellence, they act on this formulation: *Do the best you can within the time, information, and resources you have available. Gather additional information as necessary, but do act within a reasonable time.*

Both the requiring and aspiring philosophies influence how you interpret experience. Here is the choice: The requiring philosophy involves asserting irrational expectations, demands, instances, and requirements. The aspiring philosophy involves asserting rational preferences, wishes, decisions, and choices. By comparing both philosophies, you can see that each has a different "feel" and different result.

You can use the following chart to map the perfectionist requiring option with the *do it now* aspiring option. Next time you confront a challenging situation where you feel anxious and pressured, write out the requiring and aspiring directions to put what is happening in perspective. By making the contrast you can open the option of working toward the normally more productive aspiring view.

Requiring vs. Aspiring

Situation that involves performing effectively: _____.

Requiring Philosophy	Aspiring Philosophy
1. Performance demands you impose on yourself:	1. Achievement goals you aspire to meet:
2. Method of evaluating yourself if you fall short of your expectations:	2. Measure of judging your performance if you do less well than you would like:
3. Procrastination solutions to avoid self-censuring:	3. Corrective steps to gain a stronger sense of mastery:

Perfectionism is one of those psychological hot spots that can yield ground to awareness. When you recognize the requiring process, you are in a better position to shift from autocratic, internalized demands to a view where you actively express your desires and preferences to keep up with your social responsibilities and to advance your personal interests. Next time you think about procrastinating because you fear you'll fail to live up to your standards, contrast the requiring and aspiring views. This contrast maps the difference between a pressured, compelling, often very distracting perspective with one where you take responsible actions with a commitment to act reasonably and effectively.

Procrastination Complication Combinations

Procrastination complications can interact in a way to make a potentially correctable situation seem unmanageable. You decide not to face a fear of heights because you believe you would feel too uncomfortable trying. "Besides," you tell yourself, "if I tried, I'd have to have a guarantee that I'd feel comfortable." Since you don't have a guarantee, you go back to telling yourself that since you can't succeed, whatever you do is a prelude to failure and a waste of time.

As in the above, when procrastination complications blend, the combination can feel heavy and oppressive. However, you can extract the different complications to lighten the weight. Using the above example, here are several sample "doubt" questions to show how to confront a combination of procrastination complications.

1. Doubt your discomfort fears by asking what makes facing a fear of heights too uncomfortable for you to tolerate.

2. Doubt your need for certainty by asking yourself, "Is seeking a guarantee a way of delaying testing the waters for overcoming the fear."

3. Doubt your prediction that you will fail by asking yourself how foreclosing on yourself before you start proves that you can't succeed.

4. Doubt that you don't know what to do by asking yourself if there is a basic step you can take in the direction of mastering the fear.

5. Doubt your conclusion that whatever you do will be a waste of time by asking yourself how seeking a way to tackle a fear is a waste of time.

This evaluation process slows your tempo so you can consciously start to disentangle and rebut procrastination thinking deriving from complication combinations. In chapter 8 you'll learn more about the art and science of rebutting negative thinking.

Key Ideas and Action Plans

People can procrastinate for many reasons, some of which are best managed through self-development efforts. The procrastination complications and their combinations are the sort of self-development challenges that merit defeating.

What key ideas from this chapter can you use to further your plan to decrease procrastination? Write them down. Then write down the actions you can and will take to support a *do it now* initiative.

Key Ideas

1. _____

_____

2. _____

_____

3. _____

_____

Action Plan

1. _____

_____

2. _____

_____

3. _____

_____

Postscript

A developed procrastination habit of avoiding a needless fear typically has a taproot (core process) and many branches (different manifestations). Attacking procrastination at its branches weakens the roots, and what you do to uproot procrastination weakens the branches. So even if you suffer from self-doubts, second-guess yourself, and hesitate, if you repeatedly force yourself to take potentially profitable risks despite your fears, you may find that you procrastinate less when facing uncertainty. You'll build evidence that failure isn't inevitable and, even when things do go wrong, you can handle it.

In the next chapter, we'll look at a mapping program where you identify your own procrastination process and set goals for what you want to accomplish. Following that, we'll look at a highly structured change approach using the information you create.

CHAPTER 5

First Things First

Practically everyone can develop a long list of delayed activities. The fact that many of us make "to-do" lists testifies to the very human wish to stay organized and get things done. Though few of us pride ourselves in falling behind, sometimes the things on our lists don't get done.

Each of us has a special procrastination zone where we persistently put off what is important. You might feel that you are drifting through life and think by concentrating on developing a career skill you can feel better grounded. You might want to lose ten pounds and want to stop conning yourself into postponing your start-date. By targeting that primary area first, you can direct your efforts to break that specific pattern. What you learn, you can apply to another area next.

Your strongest procrastination urges can come in hidden ways. For example, if you're next challenge isn't smack in your face at the moment, you can avoid thinking about it. When you look at the omissions in your life, you might find gaps that result from procrastinating wherein you pay a price. Not finishing a college degree program may cap your salary level below what you want to earn. Fear of rejection can result in loneliness. Do you fear making decisions and live a life of inhibitions? Do you hold yourself back so as not to offend others? Do discomfort fears exclude you from savoring parts of life that others naturally enjoy? Look back over your life. What is missing that could otherwise be there? What would you be willing to do to fill some of those gaps that you believe are within your abilities to attain?

Exiting a Theoretical World

In a theoretical world, you always act effectively and do "first things first." But you don't live in a theoretical world. You won't always act effectively. Sometimes you face uncertainties and ambiguities where you have but a vague hint as to a direction. Like most utopias, the theoretical world stays elusively out of reach. Since you live in the real world where there are some activities you don't like to do, some you are uncertain about, and areas that you even fear, you may feel strongly tempted to delay what you can start doing today. That means in the real world, the-first-things-first theory frequently confronts a procrastination theory that later is better. Now you are on the horns of a dilemma. Observing this dilemma, the sixteenth century English playwright and poet William Shakespeare might muse, "To act or not to act, that is the question. Whether it is better to suffer the slings of outrageous delays, or to act productively, that is a question that perplexes the mind."

To help yourself answers that question, complete the following ten-question Procrastination Inventory. The inventory will help you to determine your procrastination trouble spots and to organize your thinking. You'll have many chances in this workbook to use the information you generate through this exercise.

Procrastination Inventory

1. Cite the main area where you procrastinate that you want to change. (Though this may be your toughest challenge, even the toughest has "soft spots.")

2. What do you hope to accomplish through mastering procrastination in this area? (Consider thinking and emotional, as well as behavioral, advantages.)

3. What activities do you normally substitute for the priority activity that you put off? (Considering this substitution process gives you the option of redirecting your actions toward your priority.)

4. What do you tell yourself to justify putting off the activities you described under item 3 above? (Example: You tell yourself you will do better tomorrow.)

5. What emotions do you experience when you procrastinate on your priority zone? (Do you feel frustration, "imposed upon," anger, guilt, discomfort, rebelliousness, insecurity, or other?)

6. What are the short- and intermediate-term behavioral consequences of this procrastination? (What do you lose?)

7. What future problems would you eliminate through breaking your procrastination habit? (Avoiding a problem can feel rewarding.)

8. What positive gains would predictably result from breaking your procrastination habit? (Is it a sense of relief? Do you obtain a concrete advantage or reward?)

9. What have you tried that you found effective in curbing procrastination? (This can give you cues as to what will work for you.)

10. How long have you been able to break the procrastination habit before returning to a procrastination pattern? What do you think causes the setbacks? (This question sets the stage for prevention against relapse.)

Your answer to question 10 defines a problem that most people face: setbacks, lapses, and relapses. If you are like most, you'll face setbacks many times before you establish a dominant, proactive follow-through pattern. But you need not stay stuck after a setback. Instead, you can re-engage what worked before, but this time with a modified plan to avoid lapses and relapses. For example, create a wallet-sized card. On one side, write down three concrete actions you can take to curb procrastination when you have an urge to delay, such as immediately taking a preliminary step to follow through. On the other side of the card, write down three ideas that are practical or inspirational that can help you shift from a procrastination habit mind-set to one where you think more fluidly and proactively.

Key Ideas and Action Plans

The Procrastination Inventory was designed to help you boost your procrastination problem awareness. You will find that you can use the results of this exercise again and again throughout this workbook. You can roll the results over to future exercises, and roll back results from future exercises to this one. It also gives you a framework to compare your personal experiences with procrastination against the content in this book. In any event, with a better understanding of your procrastination style, you position yourself to take better advantage of the information that follows.

What key ideas from this chapter can you use to further your plan to decrease procrastination? Write them down. Then write down the actions you can and will take to support a *do it now* initiative.

Motivation gives direction.

Key Ideas

1. _____

_____

2. _____

_____

3. _____

_____

Action Plan

1. _____

_____

2. _____

_____

3. _____

_____

Postscript

You can have a "rotational procrastination" pattern of starting with one major procrastination challenge, then switching to dealing with another, long before you resolve the first. Suppose you have a fear of failure that you've put off addressing. At the same time, you fall behind paying your bills because you see this as a waste of time. You have a fear of intimacy that you've put off facing. You face a binge eating challenge. You go on shopping sprees. In a rotational pattern, you start to deal with bill paying, then switch your attention to curbing the shopping trips. Before you get very far, you decide to deal with your intimacy fears. Then you go back to bill-paying issues, followed by addressing your fear of failure. Like Penelope, who continually destroyed her work while weaving Ulysses' funeral garment, the work never gets done.

In most instances, progressive mastery over procrastination begins when you take one major form of procrastination, learn to overcome it, then apply what you've learned to another area. You continue with this program until you have a solidly reinforced habit of getting relevant things done in a timely and effective way. In this process, you'll likely find that as you go forward, you will find motivation to persist.

The idea of progressive mastery in one key area is to persist, persist, persist until you've changed the pattern. But life is fluid. You can rarely count on uninterrupted opportunities to address one area at a time. If you are in the process of dealing with a fear of failure, and a bill comes due, pay it.

In the following chapter, you'll find a five-step self-development process you can use to organize, coordinate, and direct your efforts to effectively deal with the prime area of procrastination you've chosen to attack. By emphasizing one problem at a time, you are likely to gain more ground.

CHAPTER 6

Get Your Bearings

If changing course was easy, in a twinkle you'd abandon all negative habits and develop exclusively positive ones. Procrastination would not interfere with your logical choices. You'd feel like a happier human being, rebound from stressful situations quicker, and follow your curiosities with childlike wonder. But as practically everyone knows, when the time arrives to face a difficult personal challenge, negative habits of mind are formidable foes that don't give up without a whale of a fight.

In this chapter I'll provide a five-step approach for meeting the procrastination challenge. Although the plan will take time and thought to develop, you can start by sketching a skeletal set of ideas. As you think and incubate, you can add more. The main point is to define what you want to accomplish, to find ways to support the results you seek, and to adopt techniques that you can effectively execute to substitute *do it now* efforts for procrastination strains.

Five Steps to Procrastination Reduction

The five-step self-development process is a powerful way to gain progressive mastery over procrastination. The five-step way involves establishing a mission, setting goals, building an action plan, executing the plan, and evaluating the results. This approach provides a coping frame of reference that includes the types of activities to employ to moderate procrastination and the skills and abilities to develop to accomplish this result. Following this approach, you pick away at the foundations for procrastination.

Establish a Mission

A *mission* is a vision that gives direction to action. This self-development mission describes a two-phase process of 1. doing something to 2. achieve something. Here is a sample mission statement: "To express myself effectively before groups to improve my persuasive impact."

Missions deal with specific short-term challenges such as improving your expressive skills. They also can give blueprints for a lifetime challenge, such as to increase wellness through following a healthy diet and moderate exercise program. Your mission can be altruistic, such as to devote your time three hours a week to improve the welfare of handicapped children. People who consistently work to meet these missions are likely to feel challenged and experience higher levels of happiness and feelings of well-being.

Procrastination comes in different forms, and you can direct your mission to address different procrastination processes. Consider the following sample mission statements as options to exercise.

- Reduce procrastination through challenging delay-promoting negative thinking

- Face social phobias by engaging in social activities

- Eliminate feelings of helplessness by executing productive actions

- Develop problem-solving skills by attacking the reasons underlying procrastination avoidance activities

Defining Your Mission

Different people have different procrastination challenges. Because of this, their missions would be very precise, such as "complete reports on time to posture myself for a promotion and to keep my job." Some will be general, such as "To progressively overcome handicapping forms of procrastination in order to take charge of my life." But to avoid the promissory-note problem, the mission would best be meaningful and beneficial.

What is your mission? List it in the box below.

Set Goals

In 1859, U.S. Senator Carl Schurz described idealized goals when he said, "Ideals are like stars; you will not succeed in touching them with your hands. But like the seafaring man on the desert of waters, you choose them as your guides, and following them, you will reach your destiny."

Most of what we do is goal-directed. Our goals represent what we want to achieve. Setting and executing goals is one of the most reliably advantageous approaches to self-development. How you shape your goals can make a difference. Here are five goal development guidelines:

- It's important that your goals fit with your mission. When your goals involve eventually *experiencing* what you desire, you have an incentive to achieve them.

- When your goals point to a direction where you can stretch your resources to progressively master a top priority challenge, they are a motivational tool.

- Set realistic goals—ones that you can meet or develop the ability to achieve. Challenging but attainable goals tend to raise your level of motivation and the quality of your actions.

- Make your goals "mastery goals." These type of goals involve working to improve personal competencies through mastering new challenges.

- Give yourself performance goals. These benchmarks for achievements are the measured results of your efforts. Paying all bills one week before they're due is an example of a performance goal. This leads to mastery by exercising conscientiousness.

- When feasible, combine intrinsic with extrinsic goals. An intrinsic goal is one where you strive to achieve something you desire and want, such as freedom from feeling stressed about procrastination. An extrinsic goal involves doing something to get a reward or to avoid punishment. For example, studying for a test well in advance of its occurrence then reviewing can increase your chances for a higher grade. This would gain you rewards for doing well and the advantages of avoiding getting a poor or failing grade. As a practical matter, acting competently to eliminate the consequences of self-handicapping forms of procrastination has both an intrinsic and extrinsic benefit.

It's normally better—but not necessary—to focus on one goal at a time, then apply what you learned to other *do it now* goals. If you are under multiple pressures, then common sense dictates that you deal with a pressing emergent priority so that it doesn't rise to a crisis.

Make Objectives

When you break your goals down into measurable objectives, you improve your chances to progress with your mission. For example, suppose you have avoided working on a public speaking phobia, and now you want to tackle this challenge (public speaking phobias are the second most common phobia).

You can translate this goal into three objectives: 1. complete a public-speaking course at a local college, 2. research a work project, and 3. present a plan for the work project before your colleagues where you work. These three objectives are measurable. For example, if you participate in a public-speaking course, you achieve that objective. When you can measure your progress, you know that you're headed in the right direction. You also know when you have good reason to give yourself a pat on the back!

Create Goal Standards

Even if you set as your goals ones that are a bit more vague ("To exist in a mental state of nirvana"), you still can create standards. In such cases as living in a state of nirvana, after you've defined it, you should be able to measure it. How else are you really going to know if you've detached yourself from a sense of self or you lead a life of indifferent wisdom and compassion?

Suppose you freeze in front of groups. You set as one of your goals to deliver speeches before groups. You can apply emotion, thinking, and action standards as guideposts for measuring your progress. To illustrate, I'll continue with the public speaking goal example.

Emotional standards. It's normal to create standards for how you would like to feel, such as speaking without fear. Since speaking without fear is a subjective goal, gauged only on your expectations and hopes for yourself, you can create a "fear thermometer" to get a reading for your emotional temperature in the different phases of meeting a public speaking goal.

First draw a thermometer with an emotional temperature range from 0 (no fear) to 100, which is as fearful as you can be. Make copies. Use the thermometer to record your feelings each time you speak before a group. Mark the level on this gauge that you generally felt. If you are somewhere between your worst fear and no fear, mark the thermometer at 50. Keep a file of these recordings. Through reviewing these recordings, you may find that the more speeches you give, the lower your fear ratings.

Where do you set your "emotional range"? The Yerke-Dodson inverted U curve suggests a standard. You'll note that performance is related to the level of arousal of motivation. Low or high levels of arousal probably won't spoil your performance, in simple uncomplicated tasks such as answering a yes or no question. But when it comes to complex activities, the Yerkes-Dodson curve predicts that extremely low or high frustration or stress can impede your performance. For example, a high level of arousal or fear is likely to impede solving a complex mathematical problem by disrupting attention and concentration. Low arousal can lead to half-hearted efforts.

Within an optimal range, frustration arousal helps support your goal-directed behavior. I've identified this range as existing between the two dots on the curve. This optimal level of arousal is called a propellent stress or p-stress because it motivates positive action. Highly negative anxious thinking about public speaking produces a destructive type of stress (d-stress) that predictably decreases performance on those activities that are vulnerable to this form of stress. D-stress is a procrastination-evoking condition.

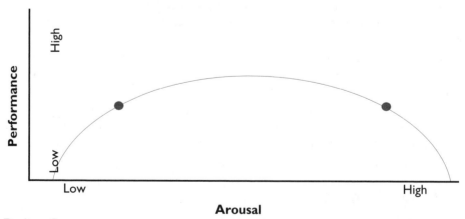

Yerke-Dodson Curve

Cognitive standards. Cognition involves thinking, reasoning, judging, believing, and verbalizing processes. When needlessly negative, these processes can contaminate clear thinking and problem solving. Cognitive standards involve reducing negative self-talk, increasing objective self-talk, and increasing your sense of control. To meet a cognitive standard for reducing negative procrastination self-talk, you take a hard look at the self-fulfilling nature of this negative thinking by comparing this thinking against its results. Then you act to challenge the negative thinking process and change the results. You'll learn more about how to do that in chapter 8.

When self-doubts filter through our thoughts they trigger our negative memories and assumptions. We become absorbed with evaluating ourselves as we dwell on lacks and exaggerate our sense of vulnerability. This distracts us from viewing what we *can* do. If you focus on what you *are* doing, you are less likely to worry about yourself and what other people may or may not think. At this point, you've met a cognitive standard for clearer thinking that leads to purposeful action.

Behavioral standards. These are the standards for the visible actions you take. For example, speaking before audiences caps the spirit of a public speaking mission. Behavioral accomplishments you achieve before you get there will mirror the objectives that you set to promote this end result. You join a public speaking class. You voluntarily speak up at least once during each class. You participate in the assigned exercises.

In setting intermediate behavioral standards, you can create a behavior hierarchy where you gradually scale your actions step-by-step toward your goal. Taking each action is meeting the standard. Think of it as climbing a staircase where you start at the bottom rung and start the climb.

When you follow this approach, each step gives you a concrete behavioral measure. In your efforts to overcome public speaking anxiety, you might, for example, start off by saying "hello" to a sub-group of two or three individuals before a formal group meeting. As a second step, you could ask a question or make a statement in a group setting. In this manner, you keep adding steps until you can comfortably speak before the group.

In following this graduated method, you would normally add a step only when you are comfortable with the preceding step. This could mean staying at one level for several weeks before you're ready for the next step. This is normally the preferred pace. However, if you find that the preliminary steps prove simple, move up levels until you start to feel manageably tense. This is a level of tension that is tolerable. Then, in ensuing situations, repeat the hierarchy up to the point of tension. Eventually you'll be in a good position to achieve your goal.

As you progress through your behavioral hierarchy, you can combine emotional and cognitive standards and measures. For example, as you get progressively better in speaking up, you are likely to experience fewer negative thoughts, engage in more positive objective thoughts, and have a greater sense of control over your actions. Your emotional thermometer is likely to be in the optimal performance range of arousal.

So far I haven't said anything about quality of performance. My standard for quality involves persisting to decrease negative thinking and procrastination responses and to increase positive, optimistic thinking, problem exposure, and emotional tolerance. I think a *good-faith effort* is a good place to start. Doing the best you can under the time and resources that you have available is a reasonable quality standard.

Overcome Goal Barriers

As a species, we have a remarkable ability to place stumbling blocks before our efforts to change. Some of these barriers involve erroneous assumptions, false goals, and unrealistic standards. Some barriers are impossible goals, such as completely avoiding discomfort. Here are some traps that waylay the unwary.

- If you set an urgent goal to eradicate a long-standing procrastination problem, you face a new challenge. Here you might think that you have suffered long enough and must now *immediately* change. Urgency leads to high arousal that often leads to frenzied and misdirected efforts. In contrast, consider taking one small step in the direction of breaking a pattern of procrastination. Then take a second step. Remember, a trip of a thousand miles starts with a single step.

- "Safe" goals are often unproductive goals. You set a goal that while easily attainable doesn't adequately address the problem. For example, you daily take a deep breath at 8 A.M. to help decrease procrastination. The deep breath exercise will accomplish little.

- Some goal standards are clear and specific yet unattainable, and frustrating. If you set a goal to awaken each day to feel positive, and never procrastinate, how do you assure that result? What if you get the flu? By setting specific but unrealistic goals, you establish a prelude for failure.

Center Your Plans

Committing to the process of *doing* makes better sense then *stewing*. Your goal plan would best describe the *doing*. Ideally, a plan includes a realistic prediction of the timing and pacing of progress.

Plans involve answering four questions: 1. Where am I today? 2. Where am I going? 3. What do I need to do to get there? 4. What alternative routes are available? Our plans help us to estimate the amount of time, effort, and resources we'll need to accomplish what we set out to do.

In a nutshell, planning is the step that prepares for the actions you take to meet the goals to achieve the mission. Plans compliment behavioral objectives, but go beyond them by including steps to remove the inevitable roadblocks that get in the way. They can include emotional and time-cost estimates, methods to manage the costs, and ways to time and pace your actions to manage the changes. They include knowledge resources about how to go forward.

Let's look at planning mechanics for overcoming procrastination-related to a public-speaking anxiety. A typical plan to profit from a public-speaking goal might include supporting objectives by 1. signing up for the class by a specific date; 2. while attending the classes, prepare brief, formal presentations by gathering and organizing materials and doing simulations before making a classroom presentation; 3. make the classroom presentation; 4. voluntarily say one thing during each class; 5. doing a post-mortem after each class by writing down fear-related thoughts and qualifying them by matching them against what resulted; 6. identify and question negative thinking that evokes anxious feelings; and 7. live through the tension.

Make perseverance and endurance a centerpiece to your plan and you direct your efforts toward increasing your tolerance for tension. If you have high tension tolerance, you are likely to feel less stressed.

Whatever plan you decide upon, it helps to keep an eraser handy. Plans, like goals, change. For example, by the time you finish reading this book, you might find worthy additions to your preliminary plans.

Execute Your Plans

How do you execute a counter-procrastination plan when delaying execution is precisely what you put off? This matter links to motivation. How does one build positive motivation that can exceed the negative motivation fueled by the fear? One method is to carefully evaluate your procrastination-process thinking and debunk it (as we've been working on with the various exercises in this book). Recognize that you'll require an effort from yourself if you intend to persist in using your critical-thinking skills to judge important situations and carry on with actions to meet the challenges that you face.

One form of motivation is conceptual. It occurs when you clearly recognize a greater form for following through than in procrastinating. Then you focus attention onto attaining that benefit. Another benefit is to look beyond the moment to see that the actions you take today can help reduce the repeated distress associated with mindlessly following a procrastination pattern. Sometimes you have to force yourself to begin, even when you feel little or no motivation to do so.

As you confront a procrastination-evoking situation, the odds are that you will feel dislike or distress. A critical part of the execution phase involves acting to follow through while staying with these avoidance sensations until they subside. By getting past the avoidance sensations, you weaken procrastination where you get a specious reward in the form of relief following a decision to postpone what you'd prefer not to do. We see this same avoidance-relief process at work with worry. When worry is followed by relief, the relief rewards the worry. This "reward for worry" event makes worry more likely to recur. As a side note, I've asked hundreds of people to tell me the percentage of the time that the thing they were worried about actually happened. Some who complained of a lifetime of worry couldn't think of a handful of examples. In those cases, "reward for worry" takes on greater meaning. This pattern suggests that they have developed worry into a well-developed habit where they make a magical jump from the possible to the probable. They can profit from learning to interrupt worry thinking with straightforward probability thinking. For example, if you worry about being struck by lightning, what are the odds that you actually will be?

Procrastination Barriers

A classic way to sabotage a plan is to needlessly delay its execution. There are many clever procrastinating ways to accomplish such delays. You tell yourself you'll deal with completing the unwanted activity—but not now. This *diversion* has two powerful sources of reward. You feel an immediate relief. This short-term reward can be very powerful. The second reward follows a gambler's schedule of reinforcement where you will sometimes totally avoid a consequence by delaying. The gambler's schedule is sometimes rewarded but more often it is not. These two rewards have a compounding effect that makes it more likely that you will make a procrastination decision and retreat with the hope that the problem will vanish or later get easier.

This procrastination decision can generalize. Say you resolve to get yourself in shape through exercise and plan to join a gym. But when you contemplate the actual actions you'll need to take to get in shape, you include comparing yourself to others in the gym. You fear that you will look bad by comparison. The idea of exercise also conjures images of sweating and hassle. That vision is unappealing. "Besides," you think, "what if I got into shape and my life remained dreary. What's the point of working for nothing?" I call this *comparativitis*, and this factor ties closely to an inner sense of negativity, pessimism, unhappiness, and procrastination in those areas where you believe you can't match up.

As an alternative to working out at the gym, you decide to exercise at home first so you can pass unobserved through the gym. This will also let you slowly build endurance. Next, you put off home exercise because you think you lack discipline. So you buy a book on how to develop self-discipline. Then you loan it to a friend who never returns borrowed books.

Negativity breeds more negativity. Although you can find many examples of people who stew in their own negativity who are also visibly productive, this is almost like paddling up stream. In general, the areas of your life where negativity reigns, are likely to be high risk areas for procrastination. Looking for ways to turn negatives into challenges increases your chances for follow through. Working to develop a challenge outlook carries a responsibility for shedding negative bias by seeking ways to determine whether your negative ideas are actually accurate. We'll pick this issue up again in chapter 8 on developing clear-thinking skills.

Evaluate Your Progress

We are naturally judging and evaluating creatures. Evaluation is a form of feedback and guidance that is a very important part of our lives. Feedback gives us a measure of change and a basis for adjusting what we do to further our goals.

We give ourselves feedback, receive feedback from others, and develop comparisons between our performances and our ideals. Our friends, families, mates, and coworkers give us feedback. But the type of feedback we feel receptive to, and how we use this information, can make all the difference.

The performance standards we set are sometimes not as important as how we define the results of our efforts. The meaning we give to our output is highly influential. If you fall below the standards that you've set to meet your goals but accept this as an inevitable part of this process, you are more likely to use the information you've gained through your error constructively to regulate what you do next. If you exceed your goal, this information can also influence how you regulate your plans.

Self-regulation as introduced in chapter 1, additionally involves comparing current states with desired goal states, then taking steps to reduce the disparity. Self-regulated learning relies on evaluation and feedback to reduce the disparity. This learning includes:

- recognizing the relationship between action strategies and potential benefits and results,

- viewing personal development as a controllable process,

- accepting responsibility for taking initiatives and following through,

- self-monitoring by listening to your inner thoughts and connecting them to how you feel and what you do,

- engaging a self-management process of goal setting, creating plans, organizing resources, testing the plan, and evaluating the ongoing results at key points of the process,

- establishing and optimizing conditions that support the learning effort by rehearsing, testing, expanding, and making actions directed and relevant,

- managing time, effort, and error issues, such as getting rid of blocks and distractions,

- seeking advice and clarifications when stumped,

- advancing self-development opportunities by making adjustments based on feedback and potential,

- generating new insights and testing them against facts, observation, and data,

- constructing truths and knowledge from objective experience.

Helpful Feedback

Problem-solving persistence is a consistent predictor of progress. Through persevering, you can come to view yourself as a *doer* rather than a *stewer*.

It's virtually impossible to rid yourself of procrastination the first time you try. It takes thought, effort, and time to identify the tools you'll use and to learn to put them to good use. The challenge you undertake will have many ambiguities and uncertainties. In this process, feedback is inevitable and can prove quite valuable.

How do you know you are making progress in curbing procrastination? There are six classic measures of progressive mastery over procrastination: 1. where persistent procrastination previously befuddled you, you'll find that you take less time to complete the activity you initiated; 2. you procrastinate less frequently; 3. in personal-development areas that you once pushed to the side, you'll persistently advance those interests; 4. you are likely to see beyond the moment to clearly understand the benefits of action over delay and then act on this enlightened vision; 5. you are more likely to get compliments about your timelines and sense of responsibility; and 6. you are likely to feel less stressed about what you're not doing and more in charge of what you do. These guidelines can tell how you are doing in meeting your overall goal of kicking your procrastination habit.

An objective perspective can help you tell fact from fiction when you evaluate your progress. An objective, positive perspective involves measuring your gains. You can see that you've made a 10 percent gain in accomplishing an objective to get paperwork finished on time over a three-month timespan. Or, you notice that you've resisted the urge to procrastinate fifteen times in the span of one week.

You can look at progress in terms of positive gains even when the negative dominates. Four out of ten correct answers on an examination is a failing grade. However, if you look at the results as 40 percent right and then think about how to boost the next "test" to 50 percent, you are likely to feel motivated to improve rather than try to make up for a defeat.

Feedback can also be negative, constructive, and progressive. Suppose you decide to work on your long-delayed assertiveness project. You're tired of acting like a frightened mouse. As a result of deciding to go forward, you start to stand up for yourself. But at the first sign of resistance to your assertiveness, you back off. You feel defeated. How can you turn defeat into a victory? You start by analyzing your expectations to see if you can find where the breakdown occurred. You figure out that you believed that once you started to act more assertively, you'd get your way. You quickly conclude that people with different interests are likely to have different assertions. However, you don't have to yield ground that is in your command to keep. As a result of pinning the relapse down in this way, you raise your level of awareness. Still, awareness rarely goes beyond the point of self-congratulation unless you put what you discover to work. You decide to modify your objectives by using the next 100 assertions for practice. As a result of this analysis and modified action plan, you no longer feel like a frightened mouse. Instead, you view yourself as a scientist looking for ways to shape positive outcomes.

Five Points to Success

The five-step program involves missions, goals, plans, the execution of the plans, and evaluation of the outcome. I've found that when people apply the five-step self-development approach to master a single procrastination pattern, they develop a skill in the process that they can apply to another procrastination challenge.

Your Five-Point System

Mission: _____

Goal: _____

Objective 1: _____

Objective 2: _____

Objective 3: _____

Plan: _____

_____

_____

Execution approaches: _____

_____

_____

Evaluation Approaches: _____

_____

_____

Key Ideas and Action Plans

To shape a mission and a plan takes thought and effort. But this is a constructive effort, one that is likely to pay dividends. Once you have a good map for where you are going, you are less likely to go in an opposite direction, and if you do, you know you have the wrong bearing and can self-correct.

Through making a plan to overcome procrastination you further educate yourself about the process. You structure a program that you can apply and refine over your lifetime. Starting now, what key ideas from this chapter can you use to further your plan to increase your knowledge and decrease procrastination? Write them down. Then write down the actions you can and will take to support a *do it now* initiative.

Key Ideas

1. _____

_____

2. _____

_____

3. _____

_____

Action Plan

1. _____

_____

2. _____

_____

3. _____

_____

Postscript

I've heard many people say that procrastination is a lack of motivation. This view obscures a variety of factors including the situation, a person's perceptions of the situation, the degree and extent of practiced procrastination habit processes, the presence or absence of procrastination complications, and so on.

Procrastination is normally a complicated process with many twists. Arguably, some people are overly motivated to act. They want so badly to do well that their overmotivation becomes disorganizing, and so they retreat and suffer defeat. Others react on impulse more than on thinking things out. Thus they spoil their efforts through an impulsive style and often find solace in diversions that feel safer than meeting uncomfortable challenges. In some situations, achievement interests far exceed a person's endurance and the person experiences a gap between desirable outcomes and the sustained effort needed to produce them.

In the following chapter, we'll look at how beliefs induce procrastination and at ideas and techniques to mobilize your *do it now* resources.

CHAPTER 7

Mobilize for Positive Change

Most of us have heard that we use a small part, perhaps 10 percent, of our mental capabilities. Yet I don't know of any scientific evidence to show that we grossly underutilize our mental processing powers to the extent of idling 90 percent of our primary abilities. We are largely actively involved in what we do, including the times that we procrastinate.

When you procrastinate, you temporarily idle your positive reflection and reasoning skills while practicing your retreat capabilities. In this state of active avoidance, you busy yourself in other ways. These delays are normally executed to "buy time," and to avoid situations of doubt and discomfort. This process is a force that requires a coordinated mobilization of your finest resources to override.

Inner events like doubts and discomfort fears can instigate a procrastination reaction. But what is your incentive to break free from your procrastination patterns? Is it a matter of personal pride? Is it your integrity? Do you want to avoid the hassles of negative consequences? Do you want to act with greater effectiveness to earn more money, feel less stressed, engage in healthier eating practices, exercise more, stop feeling annoyed by your procrastination, or for some other reason? Do you want to feel in charge of your life? In sufficient strength, any of these incentives can be the emotional push you need. In the following box, write your main *do it now* incentive or incentives:

Why I Can Do It Now

_____

_____

_____

_____

_____

_____

Now pause for a moment. What strengths can you bring to bear to support your main _do it now_ incentives? What would you need to know to boost your counter-procrastination chances? How can you mobilize your finest resources to override a well-developed procrastination habit? As you contemplate these questions, let's look at a technique for mobilizing your resources.

Optimal Performance Techniques

In the past fifty years, what's called "optimal performance training" was commonly used to support peak performances by Olympic-level athletes at critical moments where a sudden, intense burst of effort could make the difference between victory and defeat. In this training, the athlete learned to relax, conjure an image of past peak performances, then, with extreme force, act.

In activities of daily living, a continuing state of preparation for optimal performance is a tad idealistic. Much of what you do doesn't require a peak effort. How many of us have to be highly mobilized to buy a loaf of bread? But at times, you will want to operate at your best. Say that you are in a contest or you face a difficult personal challenge. You know that you can't control all the circumstances and are prepared for surprises. Still, being prepared to operate optimally, you can more fluidly and flexibly mobilize your resources for peak performance.

From a goal perspective, optimal performance has a useful set of benefits. With a mastery-goal perspective (stretching your resources to build competencies), strategically operating at a peak level can be of great personal value. The by-product of this effort will be determined by the results, but almost surely involves progressive mastery. With a performance-goal perspective, you seek to achieve a specific result such as paying bills on their date of arrival.

You can use optimal performance methods to override procrastination impulses and thinking when they start or at anytime thereafter. Optimal performance involves three stages: relaxation, mobilization, and action. You start by first putting yourself into a relaxed state of mind. When relaxed, you conjure up a peak-performance image just before you act. In the action phase, you go ahead and launch the effort from your mobilized state.

You have many options for getting into a relaxed state of mind. You can listen to calming music, take a warm bath, or picture a relaxing scene. You can think of words you associate with relaxation, such as "calm." You can meditate by sitting cross-legged and murmuring the word "one" to yourself for four minutes. You can learn to successively tighten and relax all muscle groups. Through this progressive relaxation method, you bring about a deep state of relaxation (see Davis et al. 2000 for complete instructions on this relaxation technique). You can use imagery, such as fantasizing a feather floating lithely through the sky on a warm spring breeze. You can do a deep breathing exercise, such as square breathing. Here you breathe in for four seconds, hold that breath for four seconds, breathe out for four seconds, hold your breath for four seconds, and repeat this pattern for about two minutes. Different people do better with different techniques, so you choose the relaxation technique that works best for you.

When you feel more relaxed, recall memories of times where you acted effectively. (It helps to have a list of different peak performances to call upon.) In this mobilization phase, think of what you did when tempted to procrastinate, but you followed through instead and did so effectively. For example, this could be a time when you acted without second-guessing yourself or where you faced a tough challenge and figured out the solution as you engaged the situation. Whatever past success you choose, this is your optimal performance experience.

When you reconstruct that optimal moment in your mind, it helps to connect it to the mental and visceral states that accompanied the experience. How did you feel? What did you think? What sensations did you experience? What images did you see? Through these recollections, you call forth an optimal performance moment. You now have a real experience and mobilizing feelings to launch an action. In the third phase, you launch the action.

Let's suppose that the action you want to take involves a bill you received where you were overcharged. You now need to call the company and try to get the overcharge removed. You'd normally put off facing the issue because of a potential confrontation you anticipate would be distasteful. In using the optimal performance method, you first relax, then recall a peak experience when you effectively dealt with conflict. Then you recall what you did and what you were thinking, feeling, sensing, and imaging at the time.

For the current situation, you research the charges and prepare your case prior to calling the vendor. Then you put yourself into a relaxed state of mind. Once relaxed, you recall your optimal performance experience you thought of and find that you are able to create a positive deja vu when you recall that prior experience. Then you go ahead and launch the call to the vendor who overcharged you.

You can use the following worksheet to map your program.

Optimal Performance Plan

Target procrastination situation: _____

Preferred relaxation method: _____

Relevant peak experience mobilization experience: _____

_____

_____

Action launched to counteract targeted procrastination situation: _____

_____

_____

Notes on outcome: _____

_____

_____

As with all exercises in this workbook, this optimal performance approach is an experiment where you test the idea to discover the results that you can produce for yourself. Promising results can encourage you to develop the method further.

Procrastination Benefits

Most of the people I've seen who doggedly act to break a problem habit do so because the cost of maintaining the habit visibly exceeds its benefits. But consequences vary by the type of problem habit. In the area of alcohol abuse, the consequences are physical. The person's "highs" no longer feel as good as they once did. Feeling hungover and possibly facing legal and personal problems can get to the point where the hassles are no longer worth the benefits. I think this is the most common reason why problem drinkers and alcohol abusers go through the significant strain of kicking a pressuring, compulsive, mind-altering habit of drinking.

The consequences of delay to complete course assignments carries the burden of chasing professors to present the completed assignments, to take tests, and to change the incomplete grades on your transcript. Once you emotionally see that the hassles you create through these delays add to the time and effort you ultimately expend on the project, you are likely to feel more motivated to act to correct the procrastination habit.

By matching the short-term benefits of procrastination against potentially bigger negative consequences, you might find both intellectual and emotional reasons to mobilize yourself to start the effort to step away from a well-worn procrastination rut and then to sustain the effort.

You can use the following chart as a sort of "cost-benefit analysis" to measure what you gain and lose through needless postponements. In this exercise, you compare the potential short- and long-term benefits of procrastination ("Pro") against the potential short-and long-term benefits of the *do it now* process ("Do"). For example, procrastination normally has short-term benefits. You can feel temporary relief when making a decision to do it later. Procrastination also has short-term disadvantages, such as adding practice to an avoidance habit. The *do it now* process can have the short-term advantage of increasing your follow-through motivation. It also can have short-term disadvantages, such as when the activity is truly uncomfortable and you feel frustrated or aggravated while doing the task. It can have a long-term advantage of becoming a habit of personal effectiveness.

In doing this analysis, 1. choose an area where you are currently procrastinating, 2. write the situation down next to "Situation," 3. fill in the blanks in all eight blocks by describing the benefits in each classification. Use benefits chart to create a visual picture of this analysis.

Your Procrastination Benefit Chart

SITUATION:_____

Short Term		Long Term	
Advantages	Disadvantages	Advantages	Disadvantages
Pro.			
Do.			

This costs and benefits analysis can give you incentive to make a priority shift from diversions to relevant actions. To further support this result, 1. look at the advantages of finishing the task, 2. imagine the steps you would take to accomplish the result, 3. accept that discomfort may be part of this process, 4. convince yourself that you don't have to like everything that you do, and 5. work to accept the idea that completing some priority activities may prove uncomfortable or difficult, but that it's a price worth paying.

Key Ideas and Action Plans

We are definitely motivated to procrastinate—otherwise, no one would do it. But how do you gain a greater sense of motivation to do what you feel motivated to put off? As you go through this workbook, you'll find many more ways to mobilize your capabilities to effect constructive changes away from procrastination motivations to *do it now* efforts.

To implement this key idea and action-plan approach, list three ideas from this chapter that you believe make the most sense to you in your quest to deal with procrastination. Then write out three actions that you can take to make progress. Let's start now:

Key Ideas

1. _____

_____

2. _____

_____

3. _____

_____

Action Plan

1. _____

_____

2. _____

_____

3. _____

_____

Postscript

As you probably plan to keep your garden free of weeds, you can also plan to keep procrastination in check for the rest of your days. With this life-plan, you won't be disappointed if you don't significantly improve in a day. Operating with this perspective, if you make impressive progress in a month or two or six, you are less likely to sit on your laurels. Instead, you are likely to maintain a watchful vigilance for the signs of procrastination impulses and keep focused on your goals. In the following chapter, we'll look at some of the procrastination weeds you are likely to find in your garden. Seeing the patterns in your procrastination weed's growth can stimulate you to find ways to curb their future development.

The optimal performance technique you've learned sets the stage for the following chapter where you will learn a technique to help with advanced phases of change. Even with a strong incentive to change a negative pattern and a mobilized state of mind, you can still find yourself going through a challenging process of change that involves making *do it now* a regular extension of what you do.

CHAPTER 8

Change and Procrastination

In the world of procrastination, what appears simple may not be easily accomplished. Going from where you are to where you want to be very often involves facing barriers, most of which are self-imposed, and many of which are not readily seen. But if you had the opportunity for an instant playback, perhaps these barriers would become clear and more readily overcome.

Suppose a genie gives you the master watch of the universe. With a click, you can stop time. By twirling a tiny wheel in reverse, you can put time in reverse, but only as far back as a year. Left alone, time goes forward. This power comes with three conditions. The first is that you have the watch for only one day. Second, you only can use time responsibly, and if you violate this condition, you immediately lose the watch. For the third condition, the only thing you can have gained when the trial is done is what you learned. While the memory of your experience is wiped from the minds of all others, you retain the wisdom.

How would you spend this day in time? Would you visit a zoo? Would you experiment with self-change? Whatever you do, I'll bet that you would arduously avoid procrastinating. After all, you'd immediately lose the option of continuing the experiment.

You know that the power of change resides within you and that you can exercise it at any time. But this day out of time is a special occasion, a holiday of sorts where you can try many things that are new and see what you can do. Since you are reading this workbook on procrastination, let's say you decide to shed procrastination for the day. To do otherwise, you lose the watch. Next, you decide what it is that you'd want to learn.

You've already decided that you won't procrastinate for the day. This means that you can exercise productive choices among relevant personal-change opportunities.

Whatever actions you exercise, your prime goal involves learning and changing for the better.

You realize that change is a process, not an event, and that procrastination bedevils your existence. So you try new ways of ending procrastination, and now you enter the arena of change. Perhaps by experimenting with your abilities where it is safe to do so, you can find ways to avoid facing the same procrastination barriers again and again.

Understanding the hows and whys of your procrastination involves knowing yourself. The awareness part involves important understandings about what you value, believe, and how you operate when it comes to getting reasonable things done. As to the action part, to know yourself, you have to challenge yourself. The ancient Greek philosopher Aristotle foreshadowed this idea when he noted that the hardest victory to gain is that of regulating yourself: "I count among him braver who overcomes his desires than him who overcomes his enemies, for the hardest victory is the victory over self" (Tice et al. 2001).

In this chapter, you'll learn a different route for curbing procrastination through following five phases of change. This advanced approach includes awareness, action, accommodation, acceptance, and actualization ways of knowing and doing.

Awareness

Problem awareness involves recognizing the procrastination process you follow and what you can do to change. This awareness can be simply done by putting procrastination in an understandable perspective. For example, the procrastination habit process is like a continuous-loop filmstrip that replays the same theme. The strip has many frames. Each tells a different part of the story. How many frames are on your procrastination film? What does each frame look like? How does it work to keep the procrastination process reeling? What is the message the story portrays? The answers to these questions boost problem awareness and set the stage for a positive resolution.

Make a symbolic picture in your mind to show what you do for each phase and use word captions to describe the pictorial frames. For example, the first frame in your procrastination flick can be recognizing an onerous task. The second can be like a cloud of discomfort that arises to cloak a priority activity with thoughts of retreating. The third can be a picture of what you do as you retreat. The accompanying caption can be "run and hide." In rewriting the story, you can see yourself as a refreshing wind blowing the cloud from the delayed activity. The caption to this frame can read "blowing away procrastination complications." For the next image, you could picture yourself advancing. The caption of this frame can be something like "advancing to finish the task." This combination of a pictorial image and written captions can help you to see your procrastination story from a different perspective. Here the object is to understand the movement of the endless procrastination loop.

Your Procrastination Filmstrip

Procrastination Flick

1. _____

_____

2. _____

_____

3. _____

_____

4. _____

_____

5. _____

_____

6. _____

_____

7. _____

_____

Rewriting the Script

1. _____

_____

2. _____

_____

3. _____

_____

4. _____

_____

5. _____

_____

6. _____

_____

7. _____

_____

Putting the procrastination flick information into images and captions and rewriting each to make a *do it now* story gives you a way to map a path to positive change. But most scripts require editing. With new information and experiences, you will have many rewrite opportunities.

Action

As the screenwriter, you change the film from a procrastination to an action story. In the action phase, you draw upon the "procrastination flick" awareness exercise, formalize your change strategy, and follow through. This is where you give your muscles commands to translate your counter-procrastination thinking into effective actions.

The know-how that comes from taking action against procrastination can lead to an interesting new plot. In writing more action into the script, we'll start with an "ABC" problem-solving method.

The ABC Approach

As you hone your clear-thinking skills, you use these skills to regulate the direction of your life. So let's take a look at how thinking influences procrastinating, and how to promote alternative thinking to change the procrastination pattern.

Albert Ellis' (1994) ABC approach applies to changing procrastination patterns. In this system, the "A" stands for an activating event, the "B" for beliefs about the event, and the "C" stands for negative emotions and self-defeating behavioral consequences. Ellis extends the list to include "D" for methods to dispute negative, erroneous thinking. He uses "E" to display the effects of healthy emotions and constructive actions that are the end result of this process.

Procrastination fits snugly into the ABC framework: There is an activating event where you anticipate facing something uncomfortable. You *believe* that you can better address this situation in the future. You experience a momentary sense of relief, as your first emotional consequence. But that is short-lived. After a while, your stomach feels tied in knots as you think that you now have an extra burden to carry into the future. Procrastination gave you that burden. Nevertheless, the following day, you find a new way to delay. That is the procrastination way!

Sizing Up the As

An activating event can be a situation, such as learning you have a phone call to return. It can be a school of barracuda swimming where you are diving. It can be a down mood. It can be a passing thought triggered by an unknown cue. It can be a dream—anything with the power to provoke an emotional response.

Suppose you had a job interview and a passing automobile came too close to the curb and hit a puddle. Suddenly, you are doused with water and mud. Your interview takes place in five minutes.

The splashing incident is an activation event, but it becomes inseparable from your expectations, beliefs, values, and your awareness of the impending interview. So you start with a nearly reflexive shock effect from an unexpected splashing, followed by a quick interpretation of the significance of this event. If, on the other hand, it was a hot day, you were in a swimming suit, and lawn sprayers unexpectedly started and you got sopping wet, you might have a different read on the situation. In both cases you got wet. Getting wet is an activating event.

A priority task also is an activating event. When viewed as tedious and defined as something to do later, the meaning of the task takes center stage. It is the meaning we give that forms the core of procrastination. Since beliefs are central to the ABC system, as well as to procrastination, let's take a comprehensive look at their power.

Sizing Up the Bs

We center a significant part of our lives around what we think and believe. This has been known for thousands of years. In the seventeenth century B.C., the ancient Babylonian King Hammurabi thought that by controlling his subjects' beliefs he could control their behavior. The Greek philosopher Aristotle described how people thought themselves into anger or shame. He was followed by the first century A.D. stoic philosopher Epictetus who taught that although you may not have control over events, you have control over your thoughts and will. Shakespeare tells us, "There is nothing either good or bad, but thinking makes it so." In 1955, psychologist Albert Ellis introduced what he called Rational Therapy, later called Rational Emotive Behavior Therapy (1994). He advanced this idea: We feel the way we think, and our cognitively driven emotions energize what we do.

Some beliefs are factual, reasonable, or what Ellis calls *rational*. Believing that you will have fewer hassles by following through is normally true. However, erroneous beliefs, especially the negative kind, can prove highly handicapping. Believing you are helpless to change is like walling your mind so that you can't perceive beyond the barricade.

What makes a belief self-handicapping? Irrational beliefs interfere with personal relationships, work effectiveness, self-acceptance, or similar positive results. They also reflect an altered reality. This is a state of mind that veers from truth, fact, and common sense.

Procrastination contains an apparent truth and a probable falsehood. The apparent truth is that some activities are legitimately uncomfortable. The probable falsehood can go something like this: "Another time is a better time." This mañana thinking is a form of altered reality. You create an optimistic fiction of a better future where what you find distasteful today becomes doable and possibly agreeable. The results of this thinking usually don't work out so well. When tomorrow comes, there is no guarantee that things will either get better or get done.

The more defeating beliefs are those where you expect, demand, and insist that life should be as you wish, that you should be free from handicaps, and that the world ought to be fair. While such a world might be nice, it exists as a mental drama where fantasies rule over fact. Nevertheless, hewing to these theoretical world views practically guarantees intolerance and distress. Another classic irrationality is to believe you have fatal flaws, don't quite know what they might be, but you still blame yourself for being "damaged goods."

Do you feel anxious, depressed, hostile, ashamed, embarrassed, overwrought, or worried? Each of these emotions has a cognitive signature that spells distress. When anxious, you will likely believe something like this: "I can't cope," or "I can't cope adequately enough." Thinking this way is especially handicapping when these apparitions activate negative physical arousal sensations, such as a tightening in the stomach, feelings of strain, a quickened heartbeat, and disrupted concentration.

The idea that you can do better by changing negative, irrational thinking sounds simple, but the effort proves challenging. That is because many of our thoughts happen automatically. This includes procrastination thinking. Although the concept—changing your thinking—is theoretically simple, the process takes time. Nevertheless, I find that when people know and can accept that change takes time, it takes less time. When they expect quick change, they typically hobble their ability to make durable changes.

Sizing Up the Cs

The C stands for consequences. The consequences come in emotional and behavioral forms. Insisting on a fair world where everyone follows rules of courtesy is a prelude to frustration. A "fatal flaw" view predicts feelings of insecurity and restricted and inhibited activities in those areas of your life where this view prevails.

As consequences flow from your beliefs about a priority activating event that you put off, you can still hope for a brighter future. But when you engage a timely, relevant but uncomfortable activity, the behavioral consequence is positive—you have achieved completion.

Sizing Up the Ds

Negative, irrational, erroneous, or habitual thinking that inhibits you typically results in needless restriction. These forms of thought are natural targets for revision. To make these revisions, Ellis advises disputing these ways of thinking.

In reviewing procrastination thinking, you question what makes later better. If you feel uncomfortable and act like you believed you can't tolerate discomfort, ask yourself what makes the feeling of discomfort so intolerable that you can't take it. Isn't it more likely the case that you can stand what you don't like, but prefer not to feel uncomfortable? This difference in perspective can help you to see yourself as a person who *can* stand what you don't like.

Sizing Up the Es

E stands for the effects of healthier beliefs and actions. When you think and act like you can't tolerate discomfort, you're likely to put off what you feel uncomfortable doing. By disputing that view, you teach yourself to respond by thinking that, while you certainly prefer comfort to discomfort, you can tolerate what you don't like. Accepting discomfort, then, often alters the nothing feeling, making it feel less intense and more manageable. With fewer attempts to dodge discomfort you have one fewer harassing conditions to contend with.

When you get to positive new behavioral and emotional effects, your efforts are directed toward *do it now* activities. You are likely to experience a broader range of emotions, including positive feelings of happiness and satisfaction. Your disappointments, regrets, and frustrations are likely to go unembellished by erroneous claims and demands for a more perfect world. Without distracting demands, you are less likely to feel anxious or depressed and more likely to get more done with more fun.

Public Speaking and Procrastination

Let's use the public speaking example from chapter 6 to see how you can apply the ABC approach to counter your procrastination thinking. Suppose your boss scheduled you to give a speech before a customer group. You feel uncomfortable speaking before groups. You resent the imposition. So you engage in a bit of hindrance procrastination and delay preparation. Thinking that your boss took advantage of your good nature, you tell yourself, "I have better things to do with my time."

There comes a point where hindrance no longer pays, and you know it. Now the longer you put off preparation, the higher your expectations for the quality of the talk. The expectation leads to greater delays. At the last possible moment, you start to prepare and you discover the topic is more complex than you thought.

Following a highly caffeinated night of starched writing, you call in sick on the day of the talk. You don't feel physically ill. You do worry about how you would look standing before an audience with bags under your eyes while sounding dull.

The following ABC application can help you prevent this procrastination process. Here the A is the speech, the B involves what you tell yourself to delay preparation for the presentation, and the C is the emotional and behavioral results of the delay.

> **Thinking with negative Bs is like playing with a hornets' nest.**

Anticipating the speech is an obvious A. If you view the speech as a big negative, then start doubting yourself, procrastination can seem appealing. What is less obvious are the secondary As, or the sensations that come about when you first think about giving the speech. These secondary As are consequences of negative anticipations that also activate interpretations about your growing tension. In this sense, the ABCs can get very intertwined. For example, in the middle of this churning of emotions and avoidance, the speech is like a bowling ball hanging over your head. You are aware of its presence and aware it can drop. This adds an ongoing level of stress. That stress becomes a secondary A. The secondary A evokes a secondary B, such as the belief that you can't take the stress. Now the tension escalates. Separating the primary and secondary ABC elements creates opportunities to disrupt the different levels of this procrastination process. However, there is often another complication that fogs the issue. That is the baloney you tell yourself to justify the delay.

What you tell yourself influences how you feel and what you do. In a procrastination mode of thought, the baloney starts to pile up when you tell yourself that you'll do better when you feel rested. "Then," you tell yourself, "I'll think more clearly, have more time to prepare, and my ideas will prove brilliant." But at that point, you decide you also have other important things to do, such as beat the computer in a mine-sweeper game.

The pile of baloney grows larger when later you turn your back to your fears and you tell yourself that you will sound dull, appear ill at ease, stumble over your words, and make a fool out of yourself. These predictions activate the procrastination decision to cancel the talk.

Can you predict how you would feel at point C after believing this line of thought with secondary A and B complications? Although you are probably going to feel some momentary relief from the initial decision to delay, you now face a more durable strain as you ruminate about what remains to be done.

In a state of stress, maintaining your phony procrastination beliefs can feel like you're working against yourself. It is normally harder to reject a phony belief than it was to accept it, so when you believe in your own ideas, rejecting even a flatly wrong one can meet with stiff inner resistance. Even when you have no personal investment in a familiar idea, you may resist change. If the color red is now called "weejabe," you may resist the use of this new label. Nevertheless, knowing how your procrastinating beliefs have emotional and behavioral consequences can be a powerful incentive to avoid procrastination outcomes by pushing yourself to identify and dispute procrastination thinking at its point of inception.

In this disputation phase, you ask yourself questions such as, "What makes tomorrow better than today?" By testing the hypotheses that later is better against the consequences of this thinking, you can make strides in disengaging from entrenched procrastination thinking habits.

Through disputing erroneous beliefs you strengthen your critical-thinking skills. By engaging in problem-solving actions to alter procrastination activities, you create new proactive effects. The following ABC chart gives a structure for coping with procrastination process thinking.

Charting Procrastination with the ABC Approach

You can use the following ABC framework as a tool to organize and dispute procrastination thinking. Take a situation you've procrastinated on and fill in the blanks. If this approach is new to you or you want to know more, I've included references on this method.

The ABC Chart

The Activating Event (What stimulates procrastination process thinking? For example, you have a report to write.)

Your Beliefs about the Event (What do you tell yourself or believe about the event and your ability to follow through?)

Beliefs that are reasonable (For instance, you'd prefer to do something different but recognize that you would wisely get started now.)

Beliefs that are self-defeating (Like thinking that you cannot stand doing what you don't prefer to do. You second-guess or doubt yourself. You think if the activity is uncomfortable, you absolutely should put it off indefinitely. You believe that you should suffer no inconvenience. You think that tomorrow is better.)

Consequences of the Beliefs (Emotional and behavioral)

Emotional consequences of procrastination thinking (Negative emotions that hinder you)

Behavioral consequences of procrastination thinking (The results of the delays)

Disputing Irrational Belief Systems (Challenging the thinking-procrastination process)

Beliefs that are reasonable (Actively build and support belief systems based upon the positive results they produce)

Beliefs that are self-defeating (Match them against their consequences. Vigorously separate rational from irrational elements. Do a cost-benefit analysis for each self-defeating belief. Keep your more reasonable perspective in the forefront of your thoughts and follow the directions built into these beliefs. Challenge mañana thinking and other forms of diversions so that you can keep on target with your real priorities.)

Effects of Applying Rational Belief Systems

New, healthy emotions (Positive: concern, conscientiousness, enthusiasm. Negative: discomfort acceptance, frustration acceptance)

New productive actions (Self-regulatory activities that reinforce your individual initiative, sense of competency, frustration tolerance, and realistically optimistic outlook.)

The ABC method gives you a structured way to evaluate your procrastination habit process. By following the system, you get right to the heart of the process. By focusing on interfering with your procrastination beliefs and supporting alternative self-regulatory and self-efficacy beliefs, you position yourself to shift from diversionary to purposeful actions.

Contracting with Yourself

The ABC system involves taking follow-through action, and that is the purpose of the "new productive actions" phase of the system.

Some people find that when they make a written contract with themselves, they are more inclined to live up to the contract than to cancel it. In this contract, you substitute alternative *do it now* actions for procrastination beliefs and activities.

In setting up your contract you first specify your goal, the steps you'll take, and a schedule for each of these activities. Include a reward and penalty system in the contract.

The contract is a statement of what you will do, the rewards for following through, and the penalties for delay. On the premise that most people are willing to work for smaller short-term aims than bigger long-term goals, structure your contract to include a series of short-term objectives to follow each stage of completion of a project you have an urge to put off.

As part of the contract, use a diversionary substitute activity (reading a newspaper, watching a television sitcom) as rewards for meeting each objective. If you enjoy reading the newspaper, make reading the paper contingent on finishing a phase of the task or working on the task for a specified time. Here the "substitute" activity can serve as a reward, providing it follows a *do it now* action.

Use penalty systems along with the reward system. Penalize yourself if you don't meet an objective within a designated time. The penalty needs to be greater than the temporary benefits of delay. Penalties people have used include burning a $10 bill or writing a letter of praise to a politician whose views they oppose. By following through on your contract, you avoid the penalty. Avoiding the penalty is like getting a second reward.

You gain four forms of rewards through this contracting process: 1. the short-term, intermediary rewards that follow each phase of completion; 2. the reward that comes from avoiding a penalty; 3. the reward of completing the project; 4. the mastery reward of developing a *do it now* skill to replace the procrastination habit. Consciously matching these rewards against specious, temporary procrastination decision relief rewards can tip the balance in favor of *do it now* thinking and actions.

Some people are more likely to do something for someone else than for themselves. Others are more likely to act when they know they are held accountable. To add an additional incentive, consider having a friend hold the contract and make pre-agreed inquiries about your progress.

As an intermediary step to developing intrinsic motivation for self-regulation, this "monitor" part to the contract can serve as an additional incentive. If you are socially oriented, getting social supports can really boost your progress. Eventually you'll no longer need the external monitor as you strengthen your will to progress on your own.

Here is a sample preliminary contract:

Procrastination Contract

I contract with myself to deal with my fear of criticism for thirty days.

1. I will daily admit to a mistake or fault to a family member or friend. Each day I fulfill this contract, I get to read my favorite newspaper. Each day I do not fulfill this contract, I add two days to the contract.

2. I will daily work on procrastination urges to avoid admitting a mistake or fault. I will do this when I feel an urge to duck the assignment. In this process I will challenge procrastination thinking and refuse to engage in diversionary activities. Each day I fulfill this contract, I get to watch the evening news. Each day that I do not challenge procrastination thinking related to fear of criticism, I will donate five dollars to the campaign of a politician whose views I most oppose.

3. If I complete the assignment within thirty-six days, I will reward myself by going to dinner and the movies. If I exceed the thirty-six days, I will not go to the movies or out to dinner for six weeks, and I will send fifty dollars to the campaign of a politician whose views I oppose.

Signed

Date

Witness:

Accommodation

Accommodation involves juxtaposing ideas, playing with procrastination paradoxes, and adjusting to new proficiency ideas by making them part of the way you think and act. This is a process of engaging information that is inconsistent with strongly held procrastination beliefs. In short, accommodation is the intercept point of the mind where the integration of new ways of thinking and doing takes place.

Through accommodation, you continue as your own playwright but now you integrate your story. In the accommodation phase of change, you start to put your thoughts together so that you have an emotional understanding of progressive mastery over procrastination because you have experienced the process and found it to be valid. You are engaged in an accommodation process where you mesh your intellectual and emotional understanding with *do it now* actions.

Contrasting Views

We all have contradictory ideas. Contrasting procrastination views against *do it now* views can lead to a better understanding of what's going on when you get a procrastination urge. To improve your accommodation efforts, here is a juxtaposition table that contrasts these two ways of thinking.

Procrastinating vs. Doing

Procrastination View	Do It Now View
Procrastination is too tough to change	Acting to make reasonable changes
Ducking responsibility	Acting to fulfill responsibility
Viewing oneself as blameworthy	Accepting your human fallibility
Believing an activity is too tough	Finding a reasonable place to start
Thinking that later is better	Debunking the mañana view, then taking a proactive step
Fearing failure	Desiring accomplishment
Avoiding discomfort	Seeking opportunity
Defending against threat	Meeting a challenge

In a flexible, accommodating state of mind, flipping perspectives using procrastination and *do it now* views can open options you hadn't before considered. Use this approach when you feel a procrastination urge and where you believe that an alternative view could serve to redirect your efforts toward getting what you dread done.

Goal Conversions

Suppose you face a personal-development challenge where you think, "I have no life." The more you think that you have no life, the more you feel trapped in a smog of sorrow. When you extend this idea by thinking about what you mean when you tell yourself you have no life, you've flooded your thoughts with negative associations. You hate your job. You and your brother haven't spoken for years. You have no dates, let alone a mate. You have cobwebs in the corners of your dimly lit home. "All these signs," you tell yourself, "point to my having no life."

Embedded in this misery, you can find opportunities. By converting complaints to goals, your perspective changes. What are the key contradictions in your thinking that could benefit from a reflection and reasoning review? In the following exercise, list the problems you have or negative views that encourage you to procrastinate. Then take the opportunity to flip those negative views into attainable goals. I'll give an example. Following that you fill in the blanks, where you take negatives and convert them into constructive goals.

Creating Goals from Negativity

Negative Thinking	Goal Conversion
1. I hate my job.	1. Find a job I like.
2. My brother and I don't speak.	2. Open communications.
3. I have no mate or date.	3. Make social contacts.
4. I have a cobwebbed room.	4. Clean out the cobwebs.

As you consider complaints you have about your procrastinating, what "problems" can you convert to goals?

Negative Thinking	Goal Conversion
1. _____ _____	1. _____ _____
2. _____ _____	2. _____ _____
3. _____ _____	3. _____ _____
4. _____ _____	4. _____ _____

Converting bothersome conditions into opportunities and challenges helps shake defeatist thinking. Each time you turn an emotional "crisis" or loss into a goal, you've shifted from thinking negatively to setting a positive objective.

When you start right away forming a plan to support the goal conversion, this brings you to another level of integration in preparation for action. At this level, you start to envision a positive outcome. Testing the plan creates greater opportunities for the sort of integration that comes about where actions shape your awareness. Indeed, you are likely to learn more about what you can do through action than through simple contemplation.

Acceptance

There are many ways to define worth, including how much you produce in a given amount of time and what people think of what you do. In the world of commerce, the level and quality of your production is a measure of economic value. If you are a highly skilled performer in a high income area, you'll enjoy an economic advantage. Where you have a low output, you can pay a stiff price.

In the world of self-development and self-understanding, global worth ratings defined by production are not a significant part of the equation. While you can measure the results of what you do, your general sense of worth depends on your theory of worth. So if you are going to define yourself, why not take a pluralistic view? This is where you see yourself in a broad perspective.

Although you can't just snap your fingers and reverse a lifetime of social conditioning and habitual performance-equals-worth thinking about yourself, you can start to develop a positive, pluralistic theory of worth at any time. Within this theory, you are not your accomplishments, although such things can bring advantage. You are not a memory you can't forget, although that can feel distracting. From a self-development view, you are *you*, and that means you have millions of experiences, the capability of generating sentences never spoken by anyone before, over eighteen thousand traits, characteristics, aptitudes, talents, abilities, and emotions. Beyond that, you have experiences, beliefs, knowledge, creativity—the list goes on and on. All these and more feed into a pluralistic view.

Acceptance involves viewing yourself within a broad perspective and acknowledging your strengths and imperfections and refusing to condemn yourself for your normal foibles and faults. In this acceptance phase you strive to eliminate blame excesses, extensions, and exoneration processes, while still maintaining responsibility to and for yourself, as well as acting to meet your legitimate responsibilities to others.

Our sense of personal worth further involves our definitions, beliefs, knowledge, and wisdom about ourselves. Your conscious or implied definition of your personal worth can have a strong bearing on how you think about yourself and how you direct your life. A perfectionist with a contingent-worth philosophy will predictably see their and others' worth as depending on eliminating defects and gaining success. The problem with this theory of worth is, what if some defects can't be reversed? What if some contingencies for success are simply out of reach? Does that mean that you're forever worthless? From a self-development framework, you are likely to progress more with a tolerant, self-accepting perspective than a narrowly defined negative one. In a more acceptant frame of mind, you are likely to have less to hide. You are more likely to stretch for excellence, if that is your choice. But most important of all is that you can more comfortably live within your own skin.

A pluralistic perspective gives you a wider view on yourself. For example, within the circle of your life, even when you are procrastinating in one zone, other aspects of your life continue to go well. You can recognize that some *do it now* activities are onerous, boring, or unpleasant. You may not feel good doing them, nor feel elated once you have done them, but you then have one fewer burdensome hassles.

A very important phase of acceptance involves refusing to ruminate with blame extensions over your shortcomings, including the processes you follow when you procrastinate. Instead, you admit that a procrastination habit process takes a diligent effort to alter, especially when it's well practiced and semiautomatic. Within this framework, procrastinating on dealing with procrastination is hardly sensible and may not even seem appealing.

The spinoff from this definition of acceptance is that *you need not be perfect* in your efforts to replace procrastination patterns with a *do it now* approach. If you "slip" or fall short after a good-faith effort, simply try again with a modified plan.

Improving self-acceptance and tolerance encourages, as a by-product, a state of mind free from many of the negatives that interfere with prudent decision making and sensible risk taking. This spirit of self-acceptance includes procrastination thinking—but you don't have to give in to the "tomorrow" illusion. Your theory of worth includes your strengths and willingness to use them constructively. In the final analysis, embracing a pluralistic theory of worth is a self-development concept. It does not excuse procrastination, nor causing harm to yourself or others. You are responsible and accountable for your positive as well as your less desirable actions.

A pluralistic theory of worth is a platform for change, growth, and empathic self-acceptance. It has nothing to do with moral relativism, or other views that endorse that whatever you do is okay regardless of consequences. It is as much a theory of personal variability as it is of personal responsibility.

Psychologist Albert Ellis (1994) notes that worth is a definition. So you might as well give yourself what he calls unconditional self-acceptance as that view is likely to serve you better than one of conditional worth.

An Exercise in Variability

To further clarify this theory of worth, consider that you have many traits and characteristics that don't necessarily appear in the same way under different situations. A most introverted person can behave like a very extroverted individual under the right circumstances. A normally conscientious person can go on a procrastination spree.

In the following variability exercise, you will find eighteen pairs of polar opposites. You will be marking where you generally stand between each extreme. Because you'll need to have a reference point, mark a star between each opposite that you think most likely represents your general view about you. This is your "normative" self-view. Then mark an "S" in your role as a "student." Mark a "W" in reference to your role in your work. Mark a "G" in reference to your role in groups. Mark an "F" in reference to your role as friend. Mark a "P" indicating where you are when you are in a procrastination mode. Mark an "O" to represent when you are operating in an optimal performance mode. As you will see, as situations change, so your criteria for judging yourself will normally change. This exercise shows that it makes little sense to judge yourself in only one way.

Where Do You Stand?

Procrastinating .... Effective

Self-absorbed...Externally directed

Warm .... Distant

Cautious .... Reckless

Decisive .... Indecisive

Negative .... Positive

Self-doubting.. Confident

Tolerant .... Judgmental

Fearful .... Courageous

Magnifying .... Balancing

Happy... Sad

Boastful.. Modest

Shy .... Bold

Risk-taking .... Risk-avoiding

Threatened... Challenged

Enthusiastic .... Uninspired

Social.. Reserved

Outgoing... Quiet

Conscientious .... Careless

Through this exercise, you can show yourself a general truth. You are not only one way. Even if you mark yourself in the same way across one situation, your recordings are likely to change between situations.

Actualization

You can view actualization in different ways. It can be the type of oceanic experience where you feel one with the universe. That's a nice fairy-tail ending, but don't count on that happening.

In the actualization phase of change, the *do it now* approach is regular practice. It is an extension of what you believe, value, and do. In this phase, you take what you learned and found effective in dealing with one procrastination zone and apply it to another. In this phase you've also broken the endless procrastination film loop. You've changed your script. You have a refreshing new story to tell.

How to Maintain and Expand Gains

Overcoming procrastination is a lifetime challenge. There is no resting on laurels when it comes to dealing with this ancient nemesis. Like the common cold, procrastination can recur at any time—even when you believe you have thoroughly broken the habit and effectively dealt with collateral procrastination conditions, such as worry, inhibition, low frustration tolerance, and impulsiveness.

Maintaining *do it now* gains in areas where you formerly procrastinated requires discipline. To keep the advantage you've gained requires reapplying *do it now* ideas and strategies. Admittedly, this can prove challenging when procrastination thinking spontaneously reoccurs. Often procrastination kicks up when you are overly confident or vulnerable. Overconfidence will lead to letting down your guard.

When you feel vulnerable (fatigued, stressed, uncertain, and so forth) a normal human tendency is to go back to earlier forms of thinking and acting. So if in the past, "stress" evoked a procrastination prescription, this process can spontaneously recover under stress. Remember, you will seriously test your *do it now* resolve many times.

Even when you have progressively mastered procrastination in an important life zone, relapses will occasionally occur. Say that it's a hot day. The procrastinator in you sees an opening and suggests that you can get the task done when it cools down. Now you have a choice: Follow this procrastination prescription or act to beat that procrastinator voice by engaging in *do it now* actions.

Generalizing What You Know

We can view procrastination on a continuum that goes from mild to serious. When you are on that continuum, you may find yourself in different places at the same time with regard to different forms of procrastination. You might wonder, "If I can overcome procrastination on decision making, why can't I automatically and routinely pay my bills on time?"

The process of actualization involves extending your abilities to create or meet new challenges. Applying your abilities and talents this way is part of *progressive mastery*. You may want to reach for a higher level in your career. You decide what challenges to create and how you will meet them. This self-extension involves generalizing what you know to different but relevant situations. Once you have learned to overcome procrastination in one area, for example, you can test the same process in another.

One positive change does not automatically generalize to another. But what you learn in meeting one procrastination challenge can apply to more. Thus, you don't have to start from scratch with each new impulse to delay. For example, tearing down a termite-infested shed doesn't automatically result in repairing a dent on an automobile. Both have similar, as well as different, attributes. However, once you've gained skills in using, say, a crowbar or a wrench, you have a transferable skill. But you still have to *apply* that skill if you want to achieve a result. If you want to spread your ability to curb procrastination in different areas of your life, you'll have to reapply your *do it now* skills.

The spirit of generalization is this: 1. When you gain control of a *do it now* process in one area, take this control to another area of delay. 2. Take what you've learned that applies to the new area and implement those steps. Be alert to additional activities that can apply to the new situation. 3. Observe what happens. When you need to make adjustments, play with techniques and methods to shape the results you seek. Allow yourself time to consolidate the *do it now* process in the new area. Then move to another.

Maintenance and expansion are active constructive processes. They do not normally happen automatically. To support this change, each day review how you have maintained your *do it now* gains.

In completing this chart list your accomplishments and how you obtained them. This gives you a record you can look back upon and use when you face new procrastination challenges.

Maintaining Your Gains

1. What did you do to maintain momentum for the activity?

2. How did you avoid sidetracking yourself?

3. What tools did you apply to face up to low frustration tolerance and/or discomfort dodging sequences?

4. What did you learn, or have reinforced, by engaging in *do it now* principles to gain progressive mastery?

It is easy to sit on past accomplishments. However, by stretching your personal resources into challenging new areas, you can learn more about what you can accomplish, while reinforcing what you've learned. That is the spirit of expansion of knowledge and know-how. Use the following outline to map out and assess your expansion process. First list your goal and plan. After you've executed the plan, describe what resulted. In the evaluation phase, determine the quality of the results and what you can do next to expand some more.

How You'll Expand

Expansion Goal	Plan	Results	Evaluation

Although actualization can seem like an experience that should come naturally, more often the feeling of naturalness follows working at making important changes. This is an active, constructive, progressive, propelling process. The expansion exercise emphasizes how you can propel and generalize your gains.

Key Ideas and Action Plans

Going from where you are to where you want to be involves a process. In bridging away from old, negative procrastination presses, you have to deal with them as well as build proactive follow-through skills. This chapter presented a map to mark this territory. Test it and modify it when you find a better way.

What key ideas from this chapter can you use to further you plan to decrease procrastination? Write them down. Then write down the actions you can and will take to support a *do it now* initiative.

Key Ideas

1. _____

_____

2. _____

_____

3. _____

_____

Action Plan

1. _____

_____

2. _____

_____

3. _____

_____

Postscript

Sidetracking yourself from uncertainty, discomfort, tedium, or conflict can give you a sense of temporary relief, especially when you convince yourself that you can later control the situation you now avoid. But the often fallacious idea that later is better may compound into even more interference when you're conflicted between retreating or acting. In the following chapter we'll look at this mañana diversion and many other ways to interfere with getting reasonable things done in a reasonable way within a reasonable time.

PART II

Advanced Techniques
and Special Topics

CHAPTER 9

Procrastination Diversions

Tomorrow, or some day soon, you'll get a better job, you'll communicate more effectively, you'll get in shape, your health will improve, you'll feel more comfortable asserting yourself, you'll get a few lucky breaks, many of your current problems will be resolved, accidents will happen to the other guy, your favorite team will win a championship, and your child will perform brilliantly. Does this line of thought sound familiar? If so, you're not unique.

Most people have a natural optimism where they see improvement showing up at a future time. Although often illusionary, an overly optimistic outlook is far better than a worried one.

Hope is a powerful force. Expectations that our desires are going to later be met can have a very sustaining effect on supporting a positive outlook. But they also have a downside when unfulfilled expectations lead to exasperation and discouragement. For example, in the world of the perfectionist, expectations are high and they frequently go unmet. In the world of procrastination, hope is often misapplied when you believe that the future is a better place for dealing with the events that you currently delay. When that doesn't prove to be true, "Oh well," says the procrastinator, "There's always tomorrow."

In this chapter, we'll look closely at procrastination distractions that sidetrack us from the present by causing us to look to the future for what we can do today. The distractions we'll consider include action, mental, and emotional diversions.

Action Diversions

How quickly we can sidetrack ourselves from responding promptly to even quickly resolvable situations. Whenever you tell yourself that you have to remember to do "that" later, then find a way to fritter the time away, you've entered the world of the action diversion.

Procrastination *always* involves substituting a lower priority or trivial activity for the timely and relevant one. In a procrastination mode, when faced with a pressing challenge or deadline, you do something else. Action diversions are present whenever you procrastinate.

Action diversions typically allay uncomfortable feelings. For example, let's say you need to prepare for an important meeting that you are very nervous about. Do you jump right in and begin creating your plan of attack, even though doing so makes you feel uncomfortable? No. Instead you visit the local pet store, take a nap, count the coins in your coin jar, surf the Internet, call a friend, go to a movie, read the newspaper, putter, watch TV, scribble, or shuffle pages. These are all more fun, or at least not as distressing as the talk that you put off. I call these "addictivities" when they rise to an automatic habit.

These diversions very often "daisy-chain," leading you from one activity to another in the process of avoiding what you don't want to do. They can shift your attention to where you temporarily forget what you've put off until something triggers a recall. As "activity" is often a remedy for alleviating stress, addictivities have a built-in reward for delay—but eventually there is a price to pay. Some of these prices are steep. You involve yourself in thrill seeking activities such as commodity trading or gambling to awaken yourself from a boring life. You pay a dollar price as you avoid learning more about an academic subject that interests you or developing a valued skill.

When in an action-diversion mode: 1. you recognize the need to perform the activity; 2. you associate the activity with feelings of discomfort; 3. you experience an emotional resistance as you think to yourself, "I don't want to"; 4. to escape the uncomfortable feelings of resistance, you engage a substitute activity. When this process generalizes, even minor inconveniences can trigger an action-diversion reaction leading you to put off things you weren't even worried about doing. In situations where there is a minor hassle that is part of what you like to do, this automatic action diversion process can prompt you to avoid meaningful leisure activities you once enjoyed.

Dealing with Action Diversions

Tackling action diversions is like getting to the core of procrastination. The following suggestions are targeted at this core.

1. To deal effectively with action diversions involves knowing the conditions that evoke them. When you can anticipate, you can plan ahead to short-circuit action diversions. For example, if when the time comes to exercise, you are inclined to yawn and take a nap, make a contract with yourself. Promise yourself that you will take a cold shower before taking the nap. If, on the other hand, you exercise, you can avoid the cold shower.

2. Because we juggle many responsibilities and goals every day, procrastination shifts can happen like stealth. Monitoring yourself as you are about to do a priority shift from something notably relevant to something trivial shows that you've

reached a level of focused awareness. When you've reached that point of awareness, look for the first action step you can take to follow a *do it now* direction—then quickly take the step.

3. Use a paradoxical "set-go" technique. In using the technique, you intentionally use a diversion as a prelude to constructive action. For example, once you recognize that you've started in on an action diversion, intentionally stay with the diversion for five minutes. Then intentionally use the diversionary momentum to catapult yourself into the activity you've avoided. In this way, a normal diversion serves as a coping tool to break an inertial pattern where you feel an initial resistance to confronting the activity you feel tempted to put off.

4. Use constructive substitutions. If you avoid responding to correspondence because you take a lot of time in rewrites, substitute an equivalent alternative. Speak with the person directly. If you need a record, keep notes of the conversation. Although the speaking directly is a sort of diversionary activity, it's likely to prove more productive than diversions like daydreaming.

5. A big part of the process of breaking an action-diversion pattern involves bearing the discomfort that can trigger an initial impulse to retreat. Try to substitute tolerating discomfort for the diversion. This means persuading yourself to follow through with the priority even though you feel uncomfortable. By repeating this exercise, you can build self-regulatory habits and high frustration tolerance.

6. At an extreme point of procrastination, if it isn't fun, it doesn't get done. Perhaps the most important actions to take against the type of procrastination avoidance activities coming from that view, are 1. to live through the discomfort, and 2. to press yourself into purposeful action. Even when the priority activity is not fun, it's normally preferable to get it done.

Arresting procrastination at the action-diversion level is disrupting procrastination at a critical point—where it starts. The closer you can come to disrupting a disruption, the closer you can come to meeting some of the procrastination change standards from chapter 6 where you take less time to initiate an action, less time to complete the activity, and procrastinate less frequently.

Mental Diversions

In *Gone with the Wind*, when the future looked bleak, Scarlet O'Hara remarked, "Tomorrow is another day." She believed that she would do better later.

After major setbacks, looking forward to tomorrow brings a comforting sense of hope. However, in the world of procrastination, people create a false optimism when they believe that they will brightly face tomorrow doing what they put off today. Thus said, they enter the wily world of illusion where from the point of view of tomorrow, the delays of today will be passé. This belief starts the second stage of the procrastination process where you thrust the uncomfortable activity further and further into the future by promising yourself that later is better.

A mental diversion is an intellectual justification for a procrastination delay. Telling yourself how boring and insufferable the task is going to be is one mental diversion, and believing the future will necessarily be brighter is another. A promise that you'll start later is a rational decision based on an irrational premise that typically leads to a disabling outcome.

Procrastination is rarely a stress-free solution, and mental diversions tend to put off the inevitable, while potentially making the future into an inhospitable place. Following a gratifying decision to delay, both the postponed condition and your stress rarely go away completely. Your recollections of the incomplete task are likely to break through into consciousness. The immediate relief you originally felt is likely to be smothered under a growing heap of stomach-sinking stress that you proceed to cycle into and out of. Some quickly recognize the consequences of delay and see the advantages of follow-through, rarely indulging in mental diversions. But procrastination can be so habitual that you feel like you were uncontrollably swept along by the process. Perhaps this is what is meant by the phrase "force of habit."

This mañana ploy (putting things off until tomorrow) is one of those conspicuous features of a procrastination habit. Here you think tomorrow is going to be a better time to do what you feel like putting off today. People in the mañana trap think that later is the opposite of now because later the put-off projects will surely get done. But when tomorrow comes, the project keeps getting put off to a later time until the activity disappears or a crisis appears. This is one of those classic examples where a momentary victory of delay turns to defeat as you hinder yourself from acting effectively.

Matching the tomorrow illusion against its results, you soon discover that later will either be no different than now or will likely be more complicated. For example, you put off writing a report, saying you'll start later when you will feel "into" the project. As time passes, you're expectations grow. You tell yourself you need to produce a very excellent product to show that your output was worth the wait. Now draped with an extra burden to produce a product of extraordinary excellence, you pressure yourself without taking further steps. Finally, you rush the job and hope for the best. This crisis escalation process is a common outcome of the mañana fiction.

The "contingency mañana ploy" is more complicated. Here you make one action depend on the completion of another. Then you put off the contingent activity. You have a report to write, but justify your delays to yourself by telling yourself you need more time to do research. Then you delay doing the research. You think you need to develop totally new eating habits before you try to lose weight. Then you put off developing those habits.

Where mañana and contingency mañana ploys create an illusion of hope, "catch-22" brings resolution through helplessness. When you reach the level of the catch-22 diversion, you decide that what you want you can never have. Then you quit before you begin. You no longer have to struggle. You have foreclosed on what you want. You may suspect that you really could get past your procrastination barriers, but the no-hope view can prove perilously compelling, so you don't even try. In a paradoxical sense, when you don't try, you have the hope that if you *did* try, perhaps you could do better. But that is a fleeting fantasy that you quickly douse with inner cries of helplessness.

Catch-22 comes about in many forms. Let's say you decide that you need an MBA degree to enter the career you desire. Although the MBA goal may be legitimate, you sabotage yourself by telling yourself you are not intelligent enough to obtain this degree. The result is that you don't take the steps to improve because you believe you can't win. Or you say that you'd like to date attractive people. You decide that anyone attractive is too good for you. In those rare exceptions when an appealing person is interested in you, you think they must have bad taste and reject them. This cognitive distortion (misrepresentation of reality) can feel very real to those entwined in this type of double-bind.

In the "backward ploy" you dwell on real or perceived negative events from the past. This is a variation on the catch-22 ploy. You believe you can't go forward unless you can change what has already happened. For example, you think of yourself as a victim of abuse. You believe your life is indelibly scarred by the abusive episodes. You believe you can't move forward in other avenues of life without a resolution. Since you can't change the past, you're stuck. But beliefs are not the same as facts. They are *apparent* truths that alter your perception of reality. In this alteration, they can be used to create a self-fulfilling prophesy where you use the results of procrastination actions to prove your premise that you have no hope to achieve what others seem to enjoy.

The backward ploy has varied twists. People will often complain of forgetting what they want to remember, but some also have recurrent thoughts of situations that they want to forget. The backward fiction offers an explanation to justify procrastination in personal-development areas. Here the delay may justify avoiding counseling that would help to overcome persistent, negative ruminations. If you believe you are fated to be mired in your past, and you believe there is nothing you can do to change that, you're engaging in the cognitive distortion called "defeatist thinking."

Defeatist thinking can be changed. For example, if you think you were responsible for controlling an uncontrollable event, it's useful to separate what you can currently control from what you can't. You can control the past no more than you can control the sunrise. You do have the power to shape your perspective to include acceptance for a past reality and to create a realistic optimism free of past negativity.

Challenging Mental Diversions

Say that you find that you consistently create a false optimism that later will be better. While you may also be somewhat skeptical about this promise, you nevertheless let this idea affect your behavior. To take charge of your life, you've chosen to challenge your mental diversion process through using your advanced reasoning skills. Here are four basic techniques for breaking mental diversion thinking patterns:

1. Most people don't see the implications of their diversionary ploys. That is because diversions happen as a fast-flowing undercurrent. You've developed them to protect you against threats or inconveniences. They have a certain hopeful appeal, but the hope is really a sign of false optimism. Make mañana, contingency mañana, catch-22, and backward ploys visible to yourself, and you've taken an important step forward. If you find that you keep distracting yourself when the time comes to catch these ploys in action, there is another path. Since you can normally tell a diversion by its results as you procrastinate, look for what you tell yourself that leads to self-defeating results. Chances are that you'll discover diversionary thoughts.

2. Mental diversions have their own "cognitive signatures" (telltale ideas). The mañana signature includes spinoffs of the idea, "I'll do it later." Contingency mañana involves ideas such as, "I'll do it when I'm rested and better prepared." Catch-22 and the backward ploy involve ideas of foreclosure, where you feel defeated before you begin. Once alert to these cognitive signatures of procrastination, you can engage your problem-solving resources to challenge the signatures through reason, follow-through actions, and juxtapositions. The next two items may help do this.

3. Listen to your mental-diversion voice, then take a contrary position. Flip the diversionary idea around to say that what you put off today will prove more arduous, difficult, and inconvenient tomorrow. Convince yourself that tomorrow is not better or that the task is not too tough. Admit to yourself that you will sometimes be inconvenienced, but that's life. Tell yourself that taking relevant actions that you don't like is a sign of maturity. And if you think you have to do something perfectly or not at all, label this cognitive distortion "all-or-nothing thinking," then act to do something other than the extremes.

4. Create a character that depicts the voice of procrastination. For example, think of the Wheedler as a little character that sits on your shoulder and cons and cajoles you into following the path of least resistance. The Wheedler byline is "tarry now, worry later." For example, a Wheedler ploy can include recognizable fictions such as, 1. you need to let the idea season a bit more before you do anything; 2. it should be done, but not right now; 3. you deserve to rest first; 4. give yourself a break. Now, change the Wheedler's tone to make it distasteful. In your inner thoughts, speak in the voice of someone you don't respect. This juxtaposition can give a negative meaning to a normally seductive fiction.

Emotional Diversions

People who fall into the emotional-diversion trap normally prefer to wait for the moment of inspiration where they "feel right" and can happily or effortlessly deal with outstanding social and personal activities. In this sense, emotional diversions are a special case of contingency mañana procrastination. You wait to feel motivated or inspired before acting. These emotional diversions can include avoiding situations that you think are going to be uncomfortable because you view discomfort as destabilizing. You don't want to interfere with your presently good mood. You tell yourself that you have to be in a certain mood before you act.

What makes emotional diversions unique? They center on motivational issues. In this procrastinating state of mind, you believe you have to feel motivated to act. But how many feel strongly motivated to deal with tedious details, take on a project that swells with uncertainty, or face troublesome problems?

For those who fall into this "feel right" trap, here is a paradoxical idea: There are plenty of activities that we do that we may never like to do and feel perpetually unmotivated to do. You don't have to feel inspired to get unpleasant tasks done. How many of us feel inspired to scrub a dirty floor or face an uncomfortable confrontation?

Emotional Change Steps

For those who succumb to emotional diversions, here are some "emotional" solutions:

1. Imagine changing frustrations into challenges. Here is where fantasizing can help. Suppose you have a cluttered room to clean. Imagine that you are super speedy at cleaning. Play out cleaning the room in your mind. Then, take the

fantasy and move it into action. Time yourself to see how long it takes to get the job done. (Some of us like to compete against ourselves and this strategy can make unpleasant tasks seem more like a game.)

2. Locate the physical seat of tension. When you experience mild levels of tension that you normally associate with activity avoidance, concentrate on this tension. Note where the tension is located. Is it in your shoulders, stomach, or neck? This shift in focus can sometimes defuse the intensity of the tension: acknowledging, accepting, and exploring an uncomfortable feeling can make it more tolerable. Now, use this period of tolerance for tension as a catalyst for a counter-procrastination action.

3. Face procrastination-related anxiety now. Deal with anxious thoughts as they arise. To help yourself break this procrastination catalyst, first identify your circular reasoning: "I can't cope because I'm powerless and I'm powerless because I can't cope." Next, recognize that this circular idea is a belief, not a fact. Then, ask yourself, "What are the exceptions to this belief?" Honest answers to this question can start you toward a fresh new perspective that is reasonably free of the type of negative circular reasoning that often lurks at the core of most procrastination.

4. Although most people dislike performing functions they feel uncomfortable or uncertain about, consider whether this tension would prevent you from acting if somebody offered you one million dollars to do what you are currently putting off? If that idea causes a positive shift in your perspective, act on that new perspective.

Procrastination is an example of a distraction.
If you were not procrastinating, what would you be doing?

Key Ideas and Action Plans

The power of a diversionary drive to avoid an unpleasant situation can lull you into a sense of complacency that helps build a wall of inertia where you can't seem to get going even on those things that you want to get done. Recognizing mental, emotional, and action diversions alone won't automatically cause you to reverse these patterns. But it is a start on the path of disrupting the two-stage procrastination process where you engage in diversionary activities to avoid discomfort and give yourself excuses to justify the delay. When you act, excuses are not necessary. When you deflate the excuses, the value of timely actions becomes clear.

What key ideas from this chapter can you use to further your plan to decrease procrastination? Write them down. Then write down the actions you can and will take to support a *do it now* initiative.

Key Ideas

1. _____

_____

2. _____

_____

3. _____

_____

Action Plan

1. _____

_____

2. _____

_____

3. _____

_____

Postscript

Procrastination diversionary systems represent interconnecting snares. They develop over a long time, even as far back as early childhood. Understanding their complexities and how they fit into procrastination habit patterns, is the story for the next chapter.

CHAPTER 10

Procrastination Habit Processes

It is the dawning of a new day, an opportunity for a fresh beginning. You grab your crumpled "to-do" list, brush off the cobwebs, and swear you will, this day, finish the items on the list. There is the new business contact you want to make. The leaky faucet makes demanding dripping sounds that won't let you forget them. Your exercise equipment gathers dust. Your bills lay scattered about, and you have "Organizing the bills" at the top on your list. But first, you have to brew the coffee. Hark, the newspaper awaits. Who knows what interesting articles you can find therein. And what has happened to good old Uncle Joe? It's been a while since you called. So an hour later, you're up-to-date on the family activities, just in time for the noon news and lunch. Now off to the store for that loaf of bread. Then back to the store for milk. Then back to the store for sugar, and off to the post office to mail the birthday card you forgot to mail last month. It's going to be a bit late, for sure, but your brother won't mind. Your tires look soft, so you'll need your friendly mechanic to check the air. And while there, a neighbor meanders over to chat. You talk about the affairs of the world and the latest gossip. You promise each other you'll start exercising in the gym together—but not today. Well, too late to do anything more. You have 200 channels to surf, e-mail to examine, and besides, you need to get to the bank before it closes.

Does this routine sound familiar? If so, you may already have a handle on the distinctive features of a procrastination habit sequence.

Procrastination Habit Sequences

The diversity of things people put off is legend: getting to meetings on time, losing weight, completing reports and assignments before the deadline, scheduling medical examinations, becoming more assertive, gaining self-confidence, overcoming anger, eliminating alcohol abuse, getting better organized, meeting new friends, overcoming shyness, developing computer skills, throwing out clutter, paying important bills on time, and so forth. Despite the variety of ways that people procrastinate on the things they say they want to get done, each person's procrastination has basic, common elements. You will usually start with an awareness that something needs to get done. This is commonly followed by a desire to avoid the activity, a decision to delay, a promise to get to it later, and substitute activities.

Persistent procrastination follows a predictable pattern, and the procrastination habit sequence defines this process. This sequence, like any other habit, is an automatic and predictable pattern that is something like tying your shoes. You realize you are going to wear the shoes, reach down and put them on, start manipulating the laces by pulling them tight, crisscrossing them, making loops, and snugging the laces. Each habit phase involves a combination of mental decision making and motor actions done without much, if any, reflective thought. What you do when you ski, swim, or open a door involves an automatic habit sequence that is sometimes called "doing it by rote."

Habit Controls

It's amazing how much our lives are controlled by procedural habits. These normally functional activities free our minds to do other things. The way you approach your job, for example, is typically predictable. In running a meeting, you may start by introducing new people in the group, defining the agenda, then launching the discussion. If you are a professional athlete, say a wide receiver on a football team, you practice your routes until they become automatic.

But some habits are dysfunctional. Habits of the mind where any possible calamity becomes a source for worry detracts from numerous constructive opportunities, including the opportunity to experience peace of mind. We see habits of consumption in binge eating, where you can't stop eating until you gorge yourself on fattening goodies. Depression also has an automatic quality, where negative sensations evoke pessimistic thought patterns of helplessness, hopelessness, self-blame, self-pity, and so forth. These same thought patterns can exaggerate feelings of depression.

Procrastination, like other undesirable habit sequences, can start with electrifying speed. Thereafter, you follow the same well-worn grooves of delay. You may scratch your head in bewilderment and disbelief that this pattern persists even when you decree it to stop. By identifying, fleshing out, and clarifying this procrastination habit sequence process, you put yourself in the catbird seat to break many of the links in this chain. So, we'll put a magnifying glass on the procrastination process. We'll look at the phases and stages nested within this sad progression. By the time you finish this chapter, you may never see procrastination in the same way again.

Levels of Habit Complexity

When people needlessly postpone, delay, or put off priority activities until another day or time, this process will contain at least the two ingredients: 1. awareness of an unpleasant priority activity, and 2. substituting a lower priority activity for the timely and relevant one. That's the most fundamental procrastination avoidance habit sequence. It only gets worse from there.

A slightly more complex procrastination process that includes this sequence works like this. There is a potentially unpleasant activity. Your perception of this activity triggers a negative feeling of tension. This blends with an avoidance sequence that involves substituting another activity. When compounded by delaying decisions such as "I'll get to it later," the relief that follows an assertive, affirmative, hopeful decision to delay can feel reinforcing.

In a more elaborate habit sequence, you:

1. Recognize the activity as unpleasant, confusing, uncomfortable, or threatening.

2. Experience a sense of doubt about how to manage either the discomfort or the activity.

3. Get into a debate with yourself over whether or not to follow through.

4. Bargain with yourself by promising you will do better later, then shift your attention to something else.

5. Engage in escapist activities so that you can avoid negative thoughts and unpleasant feelings. These activities commonly include letting your mind drift, racing to the refrigerator, going to the gym, drinking, using drugs, TV watching, video-game playing, chatting on the computer, or rambling on the phone.

6. As new challenges arise, you shift from problem to problem, never solving one before starting another.

7. You continue this avoidance process until you feel forced into a flurry of activity, get an extension, or quit.

8. You swear that you won't get yourself into this position again.

9. Despite a growing sense of frustration with yourself, you repeat the pattern again and again.

Let's add some more layers of complications to a procrastination habit sequence and contrast these complications with a *do it now* process:

Procrastination Habit Sequence	*Do It Now* Sequence
1. Awareness of an unpleasant activity or challenge	1. Awareness of an unpleasant activity or challenge
2. Interpret sense of arousal (nervousness, fear) as a threat	2. Interpret sense of arousal as a challenge
3. Automatically decide to divert and delay	3. Reflect and decide to engage
4. Give yourself justification for delay	4. Organize and start steps to meet challenge
5. Engage in substitute activities	5. Persist or adjust actions based on feedback

6. Concoct excuses to avoid blame	6. Complete activity
7. Equivocate on when to start	7. Maintain confidence to face unpleasant situations
8. Feel distracted	
9. Feel nagging stress over the event	
10. Debate with yourself over when to begin	
11. Feel discomfort about the delay	
12. Continue to substitute different activities	
13. Promise yourself you'll begin when ready	
14. Feel doubt and self-anger as the delays drag on	
15. Experience feelings of discouragement and helplessness	
16. Continue with excuses to others	
17. Look for ways to get an extension	
18. Rush to make eleventh-hour efforts	
19. Promise yourself you'll do better next time	
20. Repeat the procrastination avoidance habit sequence	

This contrast leads to a visible conclusion. An advanced procrastination habit sequence results in multiple complications that interfere with constructive actions. The *do it now* process is not complicated. Nevertheless, steps to implement a *do it now* process can be extensive such as working for years to develop the necessary knowledge and skills to become a nuclear physicist.

Recognizing Your Procrastination Habit Sequences

Although recognizing the pattern to your procrastination habit sequence may be a necessary precondition for positive change, simply seeing it usually isn't enough to cause you to change. But this knowledge does give you the option to interrupt the process at any level of the procrastination sequence, including its point of origin.

When you procrastinate, what sequence do you typically follow? What can you effectively do to disrupt this process and shift back to a *do it now* design? In the following exercise, identify the procrastination sequence you follow and alternative actions you can take at each point to implement the *do it now* strategy. It may help to recall a time in the recent past when you procrastinated and break it down to each of its steps.

Steps in Your Procrastination Habit

Procrastination Habit Sequence	Do It Now Sequence
1.	1.
2.	2.
3.	3.
4.	4.
5.	5.
6.	6.
7.	7.

The chief value in recognizing the steps in your procrastination habit process sequence is that once you are aware of how and why you use these tactics, you have an informed basis for making an enlightened choice. The chief value in contrasting the links in the procrastination process sequence with the *do it now* sequences is that it provides a sharper choice: continue procrastinating, or act to change the pattern.

If you decide to exercise the *do it now* choice,

1. Target a specific event that would usually evoke an avoidance sequence.

2. Monitor your thinking to identify the ideas, images, emotions, sensations, and behaviors that comprise the sequence.

3. Question and dispute erroneous beliefs.

4. Directly expose yourself to problem-related situations to help neutralize the sequence.

When you act to disrupt the habit sequence process, you take another step toward developing mastery in self-regulation. You also meet performance goals by getting reasonable things done within a reasonable time.

Key Ideas and Action Plans

You can often predict the different channels of your life where the static, inflexible, procrastination habit is a forceful undercurrent. In fact, in chapter 3 we explored the procrastination zones that were most often troubling. While in your procrastination currents, you are likely to gain a short-term advantage by delaying something you predict will feel unpleasant. But in this procrastination mind-set, you can readily lose sight of a big byproduct of procrastination. By practicing procrastination, you boost the strength of this habit of delay. This potential consequence is among the more pestilent parts of procrastination.

What key ideas from this chapter can you use to further your plan to decrease procrastination? Write them down. Then write down the actions you can and will take to support a *do it now* initiative.

Key Ideas

1. _____

_____

2. _____

_____

3. _____

_____

Action Plan

1. _____

_____

2. _____

_____

3. _____

_____

Postscript

Procrastination habit sequences serve diversionary as well as self-protective purposes. The procrastination decision to divert, for example, can spare us from facing what we think is an unwelcome discomfort. But the discomfort may be a signal to solve a problem or take a reasonable risk. In the following chapter, we'll take another step in understanding and containing procrastination through risk taking and enlightened decision making.

CHAPTER II

Decision Making and Risk Taking

You enter a cave through a hidden, bush-covered entrance at the bottom of a mountain and find yourself in a place where humans have never gone before. You follow a pathway spiked by a stalagmite border tipped with the dust of many ages. Hark—you see a light. You walk toward it to where the end of this gigantic cavern opens onto a lush valley teeming with dark vegetation. This is the legendary land of the polyped.

Polypeds are truly unusual animals. Each has six legs. While the front and the back move forward, the middle ones move backwards. The poor polyped is always working against itself.

At one time, polypeds wandered the planet. Their haven is now this spring-fed, lushly wooded, abundant land where it never rains.

No polyped is alive today who knows how or why their ancestors settled here. Each knew it was safe from all harm, except one—the dreaded occasions when spring water touches polyped fur. It is said that when water touches fur, strange things happen.

We look around and see a polyped kick up water by the side of a spring-fed brook. As droplets hit its fur, it sneezes, shutters, shakes, and flees as it works to override the redirection of its strong middle legs.

Every polyped knows that when water touches fur it causes strange sensations. This land of no rains sheltered them from that. Their only risk was when they drank from the brooks or nearby lake and their middle legs kicked droplets onto their fur.

In polyped folklore, we learn a secret. When the creature roamed the earth, it had a companion bird. When polypeds found this lost land of no rain, the bird was gone. No one knew why or when, but all believed this was a great tragedy.

Bathed in warm sunlight, stilled and silent, the land of lost rains was the calmest place there ever was. But one day, a large dust devil whirled through the middle of the polyped clan, causing one to tumble down a slope toward the small lake hidden behind a thick olive grove.

The creature alighted near the water. In a panicked struggle to avoid the waters of the lake, its middle legs, after years of struggle against the other four, had enormous strength. The poor creature catapulted itself into the water.

Now sneezing, shuttering, and shaking, the creature struggled to exit the lake. Then something strange happened. In the struggle, its middle legs turned to wings. A now surprised creature rose above the olive grove only to settle back to earth as its newly formed wings dried. The polyped had rediscovered the companion bird.

It is surprising that so many avoid reasonable risks that involve elements of unfamiliarity and uncertainty. Throughout most of our lives we've entered new situations: learning to read; being a new kid in the neighborhood; joining a club; going from elementary school to middle school, to high school, to college; getting a new job; finding a new relationship. All these events involve change. Through engaging change situations, we gain clarity on the way to developing mastery. Life also involves many familiar structures, such as the way we measure time and the languages we use. Many of the things we do have a certain predictability. Nevertheless, as the old saying goes, life is full of surprises.

Taking Advantage of Incidental Discoveries

Incidental discoveries can surprise us. Knowing what to do with them can be a mark of genius. At the turn of the twentieth century, the Russian physiologist Ivan Pavlov experimented with the salivation reflex. Using dogs as his subjects, he noticed that they would sometimes salivate before he presented them with food. His associates wanted to control this, arguing that this deviation in their plans was ruining their experiment. But Pavlov saw something different. He wanted to find out what it meant.

Pavlov made a decision to take a risk to study something unusual, leapfrogging the conventional thinking of his colleagues. And as a result of this deviation from convention, he won a 1904 Nobel prize for his discovery of the conditioned reflex.

A chance opportunity favors those who know enough to see what there is to be gained. Sometimes seeking to understand the unexpected is just the right thing to do. When chaos erupts, such as when the dogs salivated before receiving the food, Pavlov's understanding and management of these events turned accident to advantage.

Most of the decisions we make and risks that we take lead to the discoveries we make. Some of these discoveries are born within a crucible of chance. You don't know the outcome until after you've engaged the challenge.

We can mine for opportunities at any time by deliberately entering uncharted regions where we face uncertainties and must act to gain clarity if we intend to make discoveries. With the understanding we derive from our discoveries, we might find a way to control the processes we visited.

In choosing to enter situations that appear risky, you can face conflicting thoughts. On the one hand, you expect to experience discomfort and awkwardness until you get familiar with the situation, and you strongly prefer to avoid that experience. On the other hand, you know you can organize and regulate your resources so that you can ably find out more of what you can do, and the resources you can muster in this process of discovery.

In those life zones that involve risk and where you are inclined to procrastinate, your initiatives may first go toward protection. Still, making a decision to procrastinate entails risks that are quickly obscured from view. You can lose opportunities and pay a price. This is rarely your intent when you make a procrastination decision, but sometimes the result. To the extent that you choose to take charge of your life, this is a decision to enter areas of relative uncertainty in order to gain clarity. This act opposes a procrastination decision to avoid the unknown.

Decision-Making Procrastination

Decision making and risk taking intricately intertwine. If you face choices, you have a decision to make. So in the best of worlds, you weigh your options, consider their advantages and disadvantages, and use good information to render a reasoned choice that is consistent with both your values and the realities of the situation. But we don't live in a perfect world. Our informational gaps can be wider than we want. We might have too much information about one direction, only because we lack information about other options. We might prefer a safe, dry choice from a potentially riskier one with a bigger payoff. We see this play-it-safe decision in children at ring-toss games when they stand close enough to the post so that they never miss. Others choose to improve their skill by taking a greater risk and standing at a longer distance.

When you procrastinate, you decide to avoid a timely and relevant activity that you don't want to do, find difficult to do, fear doing, artificially deflate in importance, or subjectively view as risky. When such avoidance choices become habitual, you have entered the realm of decision-making procrastination.

The decision to procrastinate is normally easily made. Although the procrastination decision is often so automatic it feels natural, it is not made without some evaluation. It's like running a red light when you see a wide opening and feel safe that you'll make it. As an alternative to running the light, you might deliberate on important decisions, seek information, digest your options, and act on the basis of the best information you have at the moment. To help put this matter into perspective, let's look at a procrastination decision process and compare it to a self-regulating decision process:

How Do You Decide

Procrastination Decision Process	Self-Regulating Decision Process
Vague or confusing understanding of the choices	Clear statement of the problem
Procrastination impulse to delay	Articulation of options and choices
Judging that later is better and delay is okay	Determination of advantages and disadvantages for the known options
Rationalizing consequences of delay	Developing and executing a plan to reduce the risk of disadvantage while increasing the opportunity for gain
Repeating the cycle of procrastination	Learning and gaining from the results

The results of a procrastination decision are predictable and self-restricting. But on the self-regulating decision-making path, the results of your initial actions can be catalysts for adjustments. Unexpected events can cause you to alter your best plans. You may have to adjust your goals. You might compromise. You might change goals. Through this process, you can gain more than you originally expected.

Biasing Decisions

Making a decision that involves risk can be colored by mood, state of mind, emotion, impulse, bias, vague goals, uncertainties, fictional dangers, and other subjective considerations. Indecisiveness can come into play as a defense against a fictional problem. In this context, you have a motivation for procrastination.

Our decisions are influenced by our perceptions, which are influenced by our beliefs. When you look at life through a web of beliefs telling you to avoid risk, your views about what you can do will be influenced by negative biases. Negative beliefs and biases are especially disabling when they trigger procrastination decisions. Since inhibition and worry are common biasing states of mind, let's look at these biases and how to clear them.

Inhibition-Biased Decisions

A triangle is strong. We usually see it as a support. But a triangle can also symbolize inhibition. When inhibition and insecurity form the base of this triangle, anxiety will surely surface. When self-doubts and discomfort fear make up the other two sides, these factors are likely to interfere with sound decision making.

Caught up in this terrible triangle, people feel held back. There is no riddle to this result. Living with this triangle is like living in a swarm of gnats. Each gnat hits you with a different negative message. One swoops by labeled "fear of scrutiny." Another trails a banner reading "mistake from the past." You feel barraged by others murmuring "Watch out, you're vulnerable." Such thoughts can feel stressful and inhibiting.

Inhibition can feel like a painful restraint forcing you to silently play out a subdued role. Predictably, inhibition and procrastination about engaging in social situations strongly overlap. For example, when you feel inhibited, you are less likely to assert yourself.

When you feel socially inhibited, you are likely to feel uncomfortable around people you don't know well. You are likely to back off from asserting your reasonable rights and voluntarily give others an advantage. You hang in the background of groups, hoping no one will see you. You dread someone approaching you to strike up a conversation. You don't want to appear stiff or show you can't make "small talk." These inhibitory tendencies are like wearing a lead jacket while swimming.

Inhibition blocks and restrains through fear. But not all restraint resembles inhibition. Some forms of restraint are enabling. A healthy restraint occurs when your decisions represent an exercise of free will or the ability to follow one pathway when you could have chosen another. Say that you want to lose weight, so you restrain yourself from eating cake. You restrain yourself from driving at excessive speeds because you want to avoid an accident. You fulfill your responsibility to care for a sick friend, rather than go to the movies. Such restraints reflect self-regulation. On the other hand, fearful inhibitions involve drawing into yourself, worrying about yourself, fearing that you can do little or nothing to change, and experiencing a sensitivity to threats that will keep you close to the post in a ring-toss game. In such situations, procrastination seamlessly blends with inhibition.

Can you disentangle from inhibition by first disentangling yourself from procrastination? Unless you think that all things come to those who wait, you have the option of maintaining an inhibitory bias or changing it through engaging in the natural social situations you previously avoided. One way to get practice in doing this is by trying some stepping-out-of-character exercises.

Doing stepping-out-of-character exercises means that you do something relevant to address a problem that you would ordinarily not do. If you normally look downward, look around you as you walk. If you typically avoid eye contact, make a point to glance at people. If you avoid greeting people, plan to initiate a hello to at least three people you know each day. Ask a colleague for lunch. If you are reluctant to ask anyone for change, change a dollar bill at a different store every day for a week. If you don't pay much attention to what is happening around you, take a fifteen minute walk through your neighborhood for the next five days and on each day, look for something you had not seen before. Through engaging stepping-out-of-character exercises, you do at least two favors for yourself. You act against inhibitory feelings and behaviors by restricting them, and you cope with inhibition-motivated procrastination by experiencing and expressing yourself differently.

Dealing with procrastination comes into play in another way. If you tell yourself it would be too embarrassing to ask a colleague to lunch, ask yourself in what way it would be embarrassing. What's the worst thing that could happen? How could you cope with the worst? What is the best thing that could happen? What are the range of possibilities in between the extremes? Once you get perspective on that phase, take a risk. Ask the colleague. Test you predictions against the results. If you don't like the results, devise another plan. Try again perhaps, with someone else. You have little to lose but your inhibition.

When senseless inhibitions bias your decisions and lead to an inertial pattern of unnecessary and painful restraints, try purging this form of personal procrastination with PURRRR. You can use the PURRRR plan from chapter 1 to substitute the *do it now* approach for the inhibition plan.

PURRRR PLAN

Inhibition situation:_____

Pause	Utilize	Reflect	Reason	Respond	Revise
Stop	Apply resources to resist the pattern	Think about what's happening	Think it through	Put yourself through the paces	Make adjustments

---

Indecision leads to inhibition and inhibition leads to indecision.

By targeting areas in your life where you act with excess inhibition, you can decide at any time to put your barnacled inhibitory beliefs to the test by stepping out of character. One stepping-out-of-character experiment is rarely definitive so repeat the process. Aside from taking concrete steps to start to defeat needless inhibitions, the "Revise" part of the plan may prove the more productive.

Worry-Biased Decisions

Worry biases decision making. You are likely to act reluctantly, if you act at all, to address factors you may worry about. As a student, you worry about a term report. Your fear of impending failure is the catalyst that sidetracks you to a party. You find a way to string together other delays to allay the worry while leaving the task undone.

Leading the life of a persistent worrier, you imagine catastrophes that rarely happen. With a conscious awareness locked into a worry bias, you are on high alert. You feel a bump under your skin. You decide you must have cancer. You start to plan for your funeral while weeping about those whom you will leave behind. A friend is a few minutes late. You imagine the friend in a body bag following an accident with an eighteen-wheeler. Your boss doesn't greet you one morning, and you're sure that you're on your way to getting fired. Looking closely into each of these worries, you discover that there is a *reward* for worry. When you worry and nothing happens, you feel relief. You discover that you have a cyst, not cancer. Your friend walks through the door. Your boss tells you that you're getting a raise. But what of the events you originally feared? They end in the junkyard of abandoned ideas, only to be replaced by new notions of the same lineage.

What purpose does worry serve? Perhaps it's a problem habit to distract you and drive your self-protective decisions. If you were not worrying, what else would you be doing? Sometimes, when you look at what's missing in your life—what you'd like to have that others seem to enjoy—you can see where worry and procrastination combine to make a striking challenge. For example, what's missing, that you want there? You may find that addressing key areas of omission that you avoid due to uncertainty will bring you a bit of relief. While you can get a reward for diversionary worries, but you still don't have what you want.

An action against worry is simultaneously an act against procrastination. In the first place, directly attacking worry when you previously avoided this step disrupts procrastination over dealing with worry. But when flinching behind walls of worry, it is admittedly challenging to either interrupt the process or refocus on the self-development areas or areas of omission where you delay.

When worrying, you can feel like you're stuck in a strain of thought. Fortunately, you have many ways to stop procrastinating about dealing with worry. The "worry paradox" is a useful place to begin.

The worry paradox is this: Inherent in the negativism of worry, we find an ingredient for countering procrastination. If you are prone to worry, you think futuristically. This shows you can think ahead. If you can think ahead, shift priorities from avoidance to action, and use what you learn to adjust what you think and do. Then you will be in a position to wisely decide a course of action that is free from the sort of worry thinking that colors judgment.

Putting "What Ifs" on the Run

Worry can strongly bias the interpretations you make, the conclusions you draw, and the decisions you make. In a worried state of mind, you can find yourself entering a social situation where you're not sure what to do and instead of seeking clarity, you tell yourself "what if" stories and back away. Let's take a few extreme social-worry examples. *What if* you look foolish? *What if* other people don't respect you? *What if* you come up short? *What if* you look awkward? What do these examples of worry talk have in common? They are rhetorical questions that reflect negative projections, a sense of helplessness, and vulnerable emotional state. These are the type of psychological ingredients that invite procrastination.

In worry thinking, you have an apparent truth to examine and a potential falsehood to dispute. The apparent truth is that you are probably going to feel uncomfortable living with negative predictions. What about the falsehood? Let's say that your "what if" fear is that others will make you the center of attention, you won't live up to their expectations, and they will harshly judge you. This is a common expectation among socially phobic people. By entering a social situation that involves some uncertainty, where you anticipate moments of awkwardness, you can gain a sense of clarity about "what if" predictions.

Of course, you could ask who the "they" are who will judge you, where you got your crystal ball from, or why you feel insecure yet think that others think you are so important as to focus their attention onto you. But the idea here is to see if you can confirm or disconfirm the harsh judgment hypothesis that others will reject you. If you disconfirm the hypothesis, this means you have reasonable evidence that people did not put you at the center of attention, judge you harshly, or reject you.

Key Ideas and Action Plans

Our decisions are colored by many mental factors, some of which can be reasonable and some that can bias you in the direction of procrastination. However, the better our decision-making process, the more likely we'll see constructive risks as opportunities and procrastinate less.

What key ideas from this chapter can you use to further your plan to decrease procrastination? Write them down. Then write down the actions you can and will take to support a *do it now* initiative.

Key Ideas

1. _____

_____

2. _____

_____

3. _____

_____

Action Plan

1. _____

_____

2. _____

_____

3. _____

_____

Postscript

An obvious hotbed for procrastination to reside is in learning situations. There, a certain amount of uncertainty and awkwardness is common. Perfectionism, fear of failure, and procrastination are common enough to seem normal. In the following chapter, we'll briefly revisit perfectionism, fear of failure, and procrastination as they relate to learning. We'll look at a broad spectrum of techniques to make procrastination in learning and studying a thing of the past.

Procrastination is the habit of dragging things undone
from the past through the present and into the future.

CHAPTER 12

Procrastination in Learning

There is an old adage that the only thing we can be sure about is death and taxes. But we also can be sure of another: We will continuously learn throughout our lives. Knowledge through education helps empower your ability to solve problems. In this chapter, we'll explore how to gain progressive mastery over procrastination in formal educational settings and learning on our own.

When you take responsibility for your personal learning, you engage in *self-regulated learning*. Here you decide on your learning goal, develop a plan, execute it, and adjust what you do based upon the feedback you receive. But having specific, attainable, and measurable goals is not enough. Self-regulated learning involves goal-directed action.

Although you learn through books, imitation, and what other people tell you, in *mediated learning* you actively engage in problem solving both in simulations and in real-life situations. For example, this workbook presents many ways of viewing procrastination, information-gathering exercises, practical techniques, and action exercises. By testing and practicing these methods, you've engaged in mediated learning.

To support self-regulated and mediated learning, I start with a description of learning distractions. Then I describe information-management techniques followed by methods for reducing emotional distractions. I'll conclude with twenty-one information processing techniques.

Learning Distractions

If you are a student faced with an approaching term-paper deadline, you can exercise a procrastinator's choice. You can play video games, eat pizza with your friends, or do other things that you find more pleasurable than writing and rewriting text. Through such distractions, you temporarily avoid the awkwardness of deciding how to start, how you might compare with other students, or the uncertainty about the letter grade your effort might produce. Of course, you can later put yourself in a crunch situation where you have less time to produce a quality product. You can explain your delays away by saying you work better under pressure. But there is a better choice. Focus on the goals where you have the best payoffs.

University of Wisconsin psychologists Kenneth Barron and Judith Harackiewicz (2001) found that a combination of mastery and performance goals yielded the better result. Through seeking mastery, you persist to improve. Through following performance goals, you act to reaching a certain level of accomplishment within a given time frame. Learners can work against themselves by confounding these goals through procrastination-evoking distractions such as unfavorable comparisons and blame.

When your goal is to attain flawless performance from yourself and you worry about making mistakes, this form of perfectionism invites a dark visitor called fear of failure. The fear is that you won't live up to your standards of what you think others expect of you. This fear distracts because it prioritizes keeping a flawless image. Procrastination comes into play when you avoid the fear by putting off the learning activity. This delay lessens the time to do well and can lead to last-minute panicked learning. In disrupting this perfectionism procrastination cycle, consider that if you demand perfection from yourself and at the same time value human worth and dignity, then how do you justify adhering to strict standards that tarnish your sense of worth and dignity?

Learning involves varying degrees of uncertainty. Failure-sensitive folk will tend to either over-learn to assure high performance, or, more likely, find ways to put it off until a time when they believe the information to digest feels more palatable. This strategy is typically flawed. If you have perfectionist views with high expectations and standards and fear you'll slide beneath the standard, procrastination is a very appealing temporary solution. In this mode, you'll put it off as long as you can, then rush yourself and cram to get the assignment in under the wire. In a nutshell, the task doesn't get any more palatable over time, it just gets rushed at the end or further postponed.

There are many learning casualties who don't adapt to a competitive academic climate. You can put off studying due to a version of perfectionism I call "comparativitis," or a strong tendency to unfavorably compare yourself to what others do, or what you *think* they are doing, then give yourself a poor grade for not measuring up. Such comparisons are common to almost any society, but especially acute in those that are achievement oriented. But you also may delay because you view studying as onerous and frustrating. Then the issue is frustration tolerance.

Learners who live in a blame culture that stresses success and blames failure, early learn blame-avoidance techniques to explain away falling short of personal or academic standards. To delay negative self-evaluations, many will put off the inevitable as long as they are able. That is why so many important assignments are left until the last moment.

This avoidance has other wrinkles when you automatically use blame cliches. Many of our blame cliches have a paradoxical effect, such as when you say to yourself, "Can't you do anything right?", "What's wrong with you?", or "You're stupid." Rather than serve as an incentive to do better, these cliches are harbingers of blame, and this kind of self-talk becomes a form of task interference. Blame avoidance, then, can serve as a powerful stimulus to divert from situations you associate with fault, condemnation, discomfort, embarrassment, shame, guilt, or self-consciousness.

Subtleties of Learning

There are important subtitles to the learning process that involve the direction of motivation. If an educational goal is to help students develop intrinsic motivation (become self-motivated) for learning while using external controls (rewards or punishments given by someone else), these views can clash. University of Rochester psychologist Edward Deci (1999) points out that when you get external rewards for performances you would normally do, this can have an undermining effect. When the rewards for behavior stop, you may do less well than before. That is because external controls appear to have a negative affect on intrinsic motivation.

Your views toward external controls often determine whether you go along with someone else's schedule or resist it. Say that a professor tells you to finish your report on time. You would normally do this on your own volution, but you resent the imposition of being told to do what you would have voluntarily done. Therefore you fall into the hindrance procrastination trap and you put the report off.

School deadlines and grades are imposed from the outside. This presents a dilemma. Deadlines are effective in so far as they assure the greatest degree of conformity and compliance. Rewards for compliance can come about in the form of a good grade or praise for the performance. But when these externals are needlessly imposed, the probable result is an undermining effect, where a significant percentage of people are likely to do less than they would have once done on their own before the external controls were put into place. Pressuring people to meet deadlines they would ordinarily meet on their own volition tends to promote rebelliousness.

Information Management

Working late one night in his laboratory, a sinister scientist mutated a microscopic creature, code-named "Gulp." The tiny creature was remarkable in its ability to devour information without digesting it. With a sly snicker, the scientist opened a window and released the beast.

Gulp was voracious. It sopped in more and more information, and as it did so, it grew and grew. Eventually, Gulp self-destructed. The poor mutant overloaded on information.

Information is meaningful when it relates to solving a pressing problem. However, learning information that is not immediately useable can lead trying to learn and relearn what you did not want to learn in the first place. Boredom can set in, and lapses in attention can lead to informational gaps and to rereading the material with even less enthusiasm than before. Under these conditions, you can feel overloaded. But overload can come about in other ways. Richard Mayer, Julie Heiser, and Steve Lonn (2001) suggest that information that comes through more than one sensory channel at the same time splits attention. They also note that irrelevant but entertaining information that is part of the learning situation can also distract from the main focus.

There are many ways to reduce the information overload conditions, as well as to advance your learning interests without resorting to procrastination. We'll start with something called "advanced organizers" as a method you can use to give yourself an edge.

Create Advanced Organizers

The advanced organizing of information involves using key ideas or questions to form a mental outline to give structure to the material you plan to explore. This strategy is similar to having different labeled files readied to receive special content. In this case, the file labels are mental. The labels help the process of organizing and storing the "new" material. Psychologist David Ausubel (1963) is best known for this advanced organization method.

Through the advanced organizer method, we can devise structures for organizing related ideas. Here are a few ways to do this.

- In doing computer database searches, the abstracted articles you review often list key phrases and terms that suggest the content of the complete text. This information can give you advanced organizers. Through this process you can select the full-text articles that are the most relevant.

- In situations where a text has questions at the end of the chapter, read them first. This will alert you to what the author thinks is important. As you read through the material, some content will relate to the questions.

- Review a primer, or synopsis, in your area of study. This quick-study approach provides an advanced organizing structure by outlining the most important ideas, terms, and names.

- In circumstances where the information you seek is likely to be fragmented—it is not all in one place—you can develop advanced organizers by formulating key questions that you want answered. Then you use the information gathered to fill in the gaps.

- You can skim over the topical headings of written materials. The italicized or underlined text will sometimes point to words the author thought were significant. This can give you a general framework for learning and retention.

- Use role-reversal strategies to structure your thinking about a topic. Pretend you are absorbing the information to prepare yourself to lecture on the topic you are studying. How would you structure the lecture? What are your main points? What details would you use as examples?

Distilling Ideas from the Internet

The Internet has grown at a phenomenal pace. Through the "Net" we can rapidly retrieve information from multiple sources. For example, in the area of self-help for personal distress, you can use the Internet to learn about anything from anxiety to xenophobia. Our challenge involves determining what is relevant, finding it, making sense out of it, organizing it, and putting it to use. In this process, we cull out, sort out, and analyze the relevant information. This can be a tedious process.

Computerized information-gathering innovations have made it simpler and quicker to retrieve general information in an area of interest. This process raises the stakes. As humanity excels in its ability to generate and disseminate knowledge, we will find ourselves challenged by demands upon our internal resources of acquisition, application, and generation of knowledge relevant to our interests and abilities. The advantage goes to those who:

- Ask relevant questions that narrow the search for information,

- Sort out relevant from irrelevant information,

- Abstract common trends in the information,

- Apply reason and creativity to expand upon the information,

- Develop strong oral and written forms of communications to convey meaning.

There are a few simple operations to use the Internet effectively. These operations include learning to make a query and knowing or discovering "key words" in order to bring up information on the topic of your choice. Both of these are typically quickly learned. The intellectual process we apply to recognizing new branches of information and to analyzing results determines the quality of our searches and what we can make of them.

We build our critical-thinking skills by examining the patterns and trends in the data and culling out the relevant information based on logic, cross referencing, and reasoning. The following provides a structure for this purpose.

- Determine what you want to know and why this information is important to you.

- Experiment with key words to see what your search will produce.

- Through a cursory look at materials, you can discover other key words that can cause you to locate different branches for your search.

- Cut, copy, and store segments of larger documents that closely relate to your interest.

- Maintain a reference file for these materials.

- Some documents are worth saving in their entirety, especially those that contain core ideas and critical references. Save and use them at a later time.

- Pay special attention to documents that provide examples that you can use to support or disconfirm an idea. These are priority sources of information.

- Scan the materials to evoke associations that you might otherwise not have considered.

- Review the patterns and trends in the information. Think about what is missing from the picture. The absence of information can point to fertile new areas where you can generate the discoveries.

- Determine if the information falls into categories. If so, label them. This helps organize your thinking.

Managing Text Materials

When the information we attempt to digest is highly meaningful, there will be limits on our information processing and retrieval capabilities. We can improve our ability to remember and recall by turning knowledge into know-how. That is the process of mediated learning, where we put the information to use and observe the results.

Some courses require regurgitation of information to pass a test. Recalling facts to pass a test requires a learning strategy. Here are suggested components for such a strategy: 1. Review questions at the end of each chapter before reading the chapter. This can help highlight what the author believed was important. This procedure provides a frame of reference for the material. 2. Record, organize and summarize the key points. In that way you are doing something interactive to heighten your chances for information acquisition and knowledge development. You can also test the following techniques for purposes of improving your retention of text material:

- Tie the new ideas to anything familiar. Such relationships can help unlock the potential meaningfulness of the material.

- Look for points of repetition within the text. Some authors will repeat key points.

- Cross-reference related information resources. When you cross-reference, you look through the index of related texts for the topic of interest, then connect the information.

- Carry on a dialogue with someone who also has a vested interest in learning the material. Sometimes, through these informal interactions, a picture that was once cloudy takes on a visible form.

Getting Beyond Cramming

Despite its bad press, cramming can prove remarkably effective when short-term retention of less complex information is desired. However, surprise interruptions and distractions can snafu this sometimes positive result.

Complex materials often require significant study time. One's level of personal frustration is predictably heightened when attempting to learn significant blocks of information when rushed. According to the Yerkes-Dodson law, high levels of frustration in the context of learning complex information are likely to impede learning.

Peter postponed studying for his History finals until the night before his first examination. Closeted in his room with lots of coffee, he plowed through notes and books until dawn. Then with his caffeine eyes and examination blue book wide open, he found his mind wandering, anxiety level rising, and work output declining.

Most students will try to absorb large amounts of information in short bursts and still not suffer Peter's fate. Can you remember pulling "all-nighters" over a pot of coffee? Can you recall how you felt as you tried to memorize blocks of information to pass the test? Can you remember trying to keep the details straight just before the test? Did you feel frustrated during the test when you couldn't remember an answer you knew just hours before?

Cramming occurs when you try to memorize information within a short time. Most of us have passed examinations primarily because of last minute efforts. The information is fresher in mind so our recollections are temporarily sharper. A cramming skill also helps when we receive a last-minute assignment and must gather and report on a topic under time pressure. But if this becomes a pattern, the evolution of knowledge slows when:

- You feel little *long-term* satisfaction in cramming.

- You rarely feel success and often feel irritated.

- You limit your ability to develop long-term information-processing skills.

- Most of your learning goes into a temporary memory that is vulnerable to interference and forgetting.

Cramming, when it leads to an information overload, can result in poor decisions. For example, Alfred decided to invest in the financial markets. He allowed himself a day to pack in all the relevant information he could. So he read about puts and calls, beta coefficients, price earnings ratios, shareholders' equity, 200-day moving averages, and buy and sell signals. As the information rose in volume, so grew Alfred's frustration. He first felt stretched. Then he felt overwhelmed because of an indigestible influx of details.

Suffering from information indigestion, Alfred dumped the load, invested in Hog Belly Futures, and lost. This is a common result of an information overload—a bad decision.

Sometimes cramming is the answer. However, an alternative answer is paced learning and periodic reviews. When you review material once learned, you're refreshing your learning "savings account." Thus, if you study on an ongoing basis then heavily review the material prior to an examination, you will predictably perform better than another of equal ability who tried to learn from scratch at the eleventh hour.

Coping with the Emotional Parts of Learning

A good part of what we retain has an emotional connection. Emotionally connected information and experiences are likely to be remembered and recalled. For example, if the information is relevant to you because you are interested in that area, you'll like to know something about it because you think it will give you an advantage or because the information connects with your beliefs.

Emotions can also be distracting or represent biases and expectations that result in distortions. In this section we'll sample some of these issues and look at ways to reduce their influence on stimulating procrastination-process thinking.

Reducing Distractions

If you want to frustrate someone, interfere with their work and keep interrupting them. External interruptions include noise intrusions, such as ringing telephones or loud background conversations. Interruptions also happen when people routinely pop in to ask questions or clamor for attention or information.

High levels of frustration can also disrupt concentration and this can interrupt the transfer of information from your short-term memory to long-term memory. Obsessive preoccupations with emotional matters also can have this effect. These internal interruptions can promote an emotional overload that can interfere with your information processing and retention abilities. You can reduce these distractions in many ways, including the four below:

- The place you choose to study can improve or diminish the speed, rate, and quality of your acquisition of information. Suppose you lose considerable time studying in a bedroom where you are likely to doze off. You know you work productively in a library environment. If you put off the desk at home for the bed, then what do you tell yourself to stop yourself from studying at the library?

- We all reach satiation points where our learning and productive efficiency drops significantly. When you feel fatigued, this can adversely affect your information-processing capabilities. To avoid the inefficiencies that result when you start to fatigue and reach a point of diminishing returns, try shifting to a less taxing activity.

- Take downtime. When ready and refreshed, you will probably resume with greater efficiency.

- Moderately exercise for about a half hour before approaching a complex learning task. Exercise stimulates the production of norepinephrine, a hormone and neurotransmitter associated with alertness, attention, and concentration. Exercise also boosts serotonin (another neurotransmitter) and endorphins, the body's natural "feel good" chemicals.

Minimizing False Expectations

We normally associate learning with school work. This association can conjure images of accomplishment and confidence, as well as frustration and failure. Our positive associations predictably set the stage for meeting new challenges. However, the idea of "school work" can conjure negative images of stern teachers, threat, frustration, confinement, unrealistic parental expectations, evaluations, failure, and other unpleasant associations that serve as learning deterrents.

Unrealistic expectations can get us into trouble. Few of us would think about swallowing a whole ripe watermelon. That would be ridiculous! Yet in the wonderful, but not always realistic, world of fantasy, we can conceive of ourselves instantly learning vast bodies of information that ordinarily take lots of time to acquire and master through use. If you believe you must retain every bit of information you take in, you raise the risk of increasing your level of frustration to where you interfere with your clear thinking capabilities.

Twenty-one Time- and Information-Management Techniques

Time management and other organizing methods point to practical ways to efficiently structure time and to avoid common procrastination pitfalls. But by themselves, they do not normally eliminate persistent procrastination practices. That is because overcoming procrastination is more than a time-management challenge.

The following information-management techniques suggest a practical approach to help you reach your information management and educational goals. By experimenting with the following counterprocrastination methods, you can replace procrastination process activities with self-regulating actions.

1. Set priorities and concentrate on them. Avoid sidetracking and distracting yourself through diversionary actions.

2. The most complex activities have simple beginnings. Some of the later steps are not seen until one gets to them. Start with a "bits and pieces" approach. Break tasks down into digestible portions. Begin with the first bit in the sequence, and continue from there. Digest a few items at a time.

3. Time and pace your work. Humans have limits on how much information they can process at any time. But do stretch as far as you can without overloading your capacities.

4. Organize, record, and store important information in writing. Short-term memory is fragile. Written records are retrievable. Organize them in files (computer or paper). Scattered notes or unrelated documents put into shoe boxes can require additional searches or duplications of effort. *Keep materials organized* in a clear work area. A cluttered desk can distract.

5. Look for points of intersection. Sometimes you have several major priorities and the same deadline for each. Where priorities merge, look for common tasks that satisfy each project, and also for opportunities where you can make one effort help the next.

6. When surveying a broad range of related information, look for patterns and trends in the information. When patterns and trends in the information emerge, you can increase your sense of control over your decisions and actions with reference to that informational area.

7. Seek synergisms. Try newly discovered solutions to old problems while also applying old solutions to new problems.

8. Interact with the ideas by: 1. creating "what if" scenarios; 2. letting your conscious thoughts wander around the content by looking at the materials from different angles and perspectives; 3. looking at potential applications for the material that will allow useful information to stay while the rest drops out of awareness.

9. While working on developing ideas, keep a pad and pencil handy near your bed. Some people have insights while in the twilight zone between sleeping and wakefulness. Try this if you are likely to wake up with ideas to record.

10. Keep your lines of communication open with knowledgeable people. Present your ideas to people with good critical thinking skills. The feedback you get can help you flesh out the issue, as well as add to your knowledge and critical-thinking skills.

11. Work where your efforts are predictably more productive. People who study in library settings will predictably concentrate for longer time periods than those who study lying in bed where the cues for sleep are present.

12. Should you schedule activities such as photocopying materials, filing, or downloading information during low energy periods? Sure. Then it follows that during peak periods of mental efficiency, you should evaluate and use complex

information. Plan, solve problems, generate text, or organize yourself to prepare for when you will put the knowledge and information to use.

13. If you have a very busy schedule take time off when feasible for *revitalization* and *remotivation*, such as playing a sport, exercising, reading for pleasure, gardening—anything productive that proves invigorating and relaxing. Take time for creative loafing. This is time where you let your mind wander. You might find that periodically you can come up with new insights during this kind of downtime.

14. Periodically review information. By reexamining key concepts, you can posture yourself to discover ideas you may not at first have seen.

15. After long periods of concentration, you may get too close to the material you are developing and miss the obvious. Get some distance. Allow time between revisions of the knowledge materials you are creating.

16. Change the medium. If you are writing using a computer, edit your work using a hard copy. Working with words on a screen, then words on paper, can add novelty to your efforts. Viewing the same materials from different angles can create conditions whereby you sooner see correctable redundancies and gaps in the information.

17. Separate theories that predict from those that sound good but have little predictive value. Theories may seem solid in the world of ideas, but are they practical? Do they fit with experience? Do they predict future occurrences? Such questions can help you to maintain a practical, commonsense perspective.

18. When considering a new approach, walk yourself through the paces. How will the method work in practice? What is the first step? Second?

19. Monitor your progress and adapt your system to changing conditions. For example, keep a log for measuring the effects of your choices and judgments. Although this process can prove uncomfortable (most of us have illusions of insight and judgment and take if for granted we are correct, even if we're making the wrong moves), reality can be a surprisingly effective teacher and we can profitably use "good information" to shape our future responses.

20. Keep notes that can jog your memory for what you think is important to later recall. Notes are effective when reviewed, but rarely helpful when taken without a later review. They compensate for our normally fallible memories.

21. Try to find humor in some of the more serious things that you do. This will help you to keep your efforts lighthearted and productive.

Key Ideas and Action Plans

The famous eighteenth-century philosopher Immanuel Kant's ideas have carried through the centuries; yet, he never traveled more than a few miles from the village in which he was born. So it's not the setting or availability of ideas that alone that can make a difference. It is what you generate by using your mind as a creative tool. In your quest for self-knowledge, you never have to travel far.

What key ideas from this chapter can you use to further your plan to decrease procrastination? Write them down. Then write down the actions you can and will take to support a *do it now* initiative.

Key Ideas

1. _____

_____

2. _____

_____

3. _____

_____

Action Plan

1. _____

_____

2. _____

_____

3. _____

_____

Postscript

In this chapter we looked at ways to sharpen the way we think and to follow through with meeting educational objectives. In the next, we'll look at how to get and stay healthy and fit. Although this focus is useful for it's own sake, you also are less likely to procrastinate on learning when you have your health under control.

CHAPTER 13

Exercise, Weight, and Stress

New Year's is a time for resolutions. So at that time of year, you resolve to get your bills paid on time, clean your closet, and complete reports on schedule. You promise yourself you'll daily dust and wash dishes and make your obligatory telephone calls without delay. But such resolutions rarely last beyond the day we make them. Why? Seeing these resolutions as demons of duty, you might later wince at the thought of doing them, feel oppressed by them, and avoid them.

Among the more common New Year's resolutions we find health activities, such as losing weight, exercising, and reducing stress. Following these meaningful health resolutions, many still back off. Do they lack motivation? More likely, they lack a plan.

There is nothing magical about New Year's. The tasks you once put off, you can start at any time of the year. The challenge, however, is defining your goal in measurable terms, setting a strong plan, and executing the plan well by also effectively dealing with procrastination diversions. It appears that the breakdown occurs for many at the planning stage. The idea is there but the plan is either too sketchy or doesn't include a way to keep procrastination at bay.

Instead of waiting for New Year's, we'll look at how to start and sustain the necessary effort to achieve three prime health goals of moderate exercise, weight control, and stress reduction. The approach for directing effort to act effectively in each area involves a different twist on putting a restraint on the procrastination habit process sequence. With some creative adjustments, you can apply the self-regulating approach to take advantage of these positive health practices to help curb a problem habit. For example, if you feel plagued by a smoking habit or drink excessively, these are important health issues to address. You can take ideas from the weight-control part of this chapter to get started on breaking such problem habits.

In the pages that immediately follow, we'll look at how to get beyond the procrastination barriers that stand between where you are and where you want to be. We'll look at what you can do to promote the habits you want to develop. So if you count yourself among those who can benefit from making health improvements, let's get started.

The Approach

Despite the volumes written on how to get control of your diet, exercise more, and decrease needless stress, the statistics remain grim. Relapse rates are legend. Are there better ways to approach these challenges? This chapter describes a counter-procrastination and accomplishment-maintenance approach for dealing with these three health procrastination issues.

Including procrastination-reduction methods into your long-term health plans can prove advantageous, providing you apply them and maintain them. At the least, it makes sense to rule out procrastination as an interfering factor.

I'll describe conditions that contribute to procrastination in these areas. But if you want to get information on empirically validated health routines, check for abstracts of the scientific literature in your local library or visit U.S. government health sites on the Internet, such as the National Institute of Health. A trip to your primary-care physician also is in order if you undertake an exercise program. To supplement your nutritional planning perhaps your doctor can suggest appropriate goals and review the plan. The more accurate your information, the better your choices.

Get and Stay Fit

You look at yourself in the mirror and don't like the shape your body has taken. For a moment, you envision yourself trim, firm, and powerful. So you decide to live the vision. You join a health facility and start an exercise routine. But the valiant hope for a positive outcome soon withers when you tire of sweating, feeling winded, and you see no quick changes. You muse, "There has to be a better way." Then you start to delay, figuring that exercise is for another day. You might justify this delay in many ways. "Hey," you say, "this isn't fun. It also isn't fair. This exercise is too much work. Others look like they are in better shape than me. I need to get firm before I return."

Rather than blame yourself for frittering away money on the gym, you sugarcoat your avoidance impulses by telling yourself something like this, "The health club members look elitist and snobbish. I'll have nothing further to do with that crowd." (However, you are not there to win a popularity contest, or to interact with the other members.) To save face with yourself, you resolve to work out at your home, get into shape, then return to the gym. Then you don't exercise at home. It seems like there is always too much to do. Contingency mañana strikes again.

Motivating Yourself for Change

Between 40 to 65 percent of people will drop out of an exercise program within three to six months after they started. The numbers get worse over a period of a year. Compared to those who start, there are many more contemplating other forms of exercise programs. Some might tenuously begin to walk around their neighborhood, and after a rainy day or two, put off the project. Others follow TV aerobic programs or follow instructions from a a videotape only to eventually switch channels or shelve the tape. Sure, you might feel emotionally pumped for a brief time by the inspirational talk and testimonials by upbeat marketing personalities. But then comes the work. You can quickly find that you don't smile like the shapely, well-developed icons that appear on the screen. Soon enough, pep talks fail to inspire.

If you are one of the millions who would like to get into an exercise routine but have previously fallen into a p-factor trap, here is some information that can reinforce your determination to start and sustain the necessary effort. It helps to start with a clear and reasonable fitness goal and measurable objectives. It normally helps to review the advantages and disadvantages of the type of exercise program that has the greatest appeal. This includes what kind of impact the exercise program is likely to have on you. What are some of the side benefits? How much time is weekly required to make and sustain the gains you want? How can you handle times when you feel like quitting?

You may have read a dozen books about the benefits of exercise, spoken to experts on this topic, and carefully researched the types of programs recommended. Meanwhile, you tell yourself that you'll soon begin. You likely already have good reasons to start. If you generally think that exercise is good but lack some of the details as to health benefits, you may delay for lack of the specifics. Moderate, regular exercise is associated with a number of useful benefits. It correlates with a reduced cholesterol level, and this is typically helpful for coronary health. Exercise is a serotonin booster. This neurochemical helps decrease depression. (Exercise appears to reduce depressive symptoms.) Exercise is associated with increases in enkephalin and beta-endorphins that are associated with feelings of confidence and well-being. Moderate exercise correlates with stress resistance. It correlates with better concentration for several hours after you exercise. It correlates with lower blood pressure, slower pulse rate, and aids in the metabolism of carbohydrates and fats. The preliminary evidence for exercise as an immune-system booster is encouraging in the sense that it appears to have some positive effects on the incidence, severity, and duration of infectious or malignant disease.

The health benefits described in the scientific literature can be used to make a compelling case for starting and sustaining an exercise program. Beyond that, you have the aesthetic benefits of an improved appearance and a probable lift in general energy and clear thinking.

From a mental health perspective, if someone came to me depressed, and I was restricted to giving only one piece of advice, I'd recommend exercise. I could confidently make a statistical argument that if the person started and sustained an exercise program while depressed (admittedly a challenging thing to do), within about six weeks, we'd see a positive mood change. But of course, there are caveats. Individual differences, history, experiences, and life circumstances can come together to make this part of a change plan more or less potent than predicted.

What does it take to benefit from exercise? In general, a reasonable exercise program typically involves about a thirty-minute workout three times a week where you keep your heart rate within an acceptable range for your age and condition.

Starting and Sustaining the Effort

Practically everyone at one time or another starts an exercise program, and sustains it for varying time periods, quits, then possibly starts again at a later time and sometimes for different reasons. Although some find exercising fun, I suspect that they are in the minority.

You can start an exercise routine anytime, even now by jogging-in-place. *Sustaining* an exercise program is a challenge. You can always find a reason to delay or to quit. Following through at a health club can be an inconvenience when you have to drive to get there. Exercising at home, by yourself, can prove challenging to sustain when you have distractions, such as a ringing phone or a crying child. Weather conditions can temporarily discourage outside exercise. Indeed, it's easy to find ways to put off exercising. If you fall into this trap, blaming yourself for letting yourself down on an exercise plan normally does more harm than good. Negative blame exercises detract from problem-solving. Double troubles, such as blaming yourself for blaming yourself, only make it worse. Blame and double troubles are a lot of distracting noise. Facing the challenge because it is the responsible thing to do will help you follow through.

To assist you in developing your own program for starting and sustaining an exercise program, I'll deviate somewhat from what I typically do to describe problem-solving options by sharing a personal experience. With some temporary interruptions, I have exercised two to five times a week for the past twenty-five years.

Although some doubtlessly enjoy exercising, I don't count myself among that group. But I know that exercising is a wise and useful activity to follow. So I force myself to go to the gym on days when I'd prefer to stay home. I exercise to gain benefits and to avoid health risks that come from a sedentary lifestyle. I'm pretty stoic about the process. I accept it as part of my routine.

What have I learned in the past twenty-five years about exercising? There are times when I think of alternatives to do. I've had times when I try to pull a fast one by telling myself that I feel too tired to workout, and that I can delay until I feel rested. Fortunately, this is a relatively rare occurrence, but it does happen. When it does, I practically never take that bunk seriously.

While it is sometimes true that I feel tired or fatigued, I don't legitimatize procrastination self-talk, such as I need to wait until later. Instead, I refocus on externals, such as getting into my car, starting it, driving to the gym, and exercising.

There are some days that I will cut back on the amount of weight I lift, or the time and level I set on a treadmill. About once every month or so I genuinely feel less energetic. I find no need to push myself to the limits of my capacity on such days. This evens out because I'll extend what I normally do on other days.

I have yet to find an easy way to go through the routines. However, I find it useful to create novelty within a predictable routine. I will vary the times and days that I exercise. I'll mix up the routine by starting at different places on the equipment. To make it somewhat enjoyable, I will sometimes create games. I'll view the exercise equipment as amusement park activities. Sometimes this helps. At times I have met people at the facility, and this company was helpful. At other times, these opportunities were not available, and I entertained myself. Sometimes I watch the news while on the treadmill, and at other times I think about what I will say in my next book as I go through the various routines. Otherwise, I make myself aware of what is happening around me. I listen for new sounds, and see if I can't see something I had not seen before. This makes time pass faster. Some days I'll think about going a minute more, then another minute, and continue this until I complete my routine. I find that I sometimes get a second wind, and then breeze through the rest. I will generally challenge myself by using the heaviest weights possible for the equipment I use because I feel satisfaction in that accomplishment. I am reluctant to lose my ability to act at that level, but I understand that age will eventually naturally cause a reduction in the amount of weight that I press.

There is no one universal training method to follow to get and stay in shape. The methods you choose depend on many things, such as your physique, goals, and what you are more likely to enjoy doing more. Your choice depends on what you want to accomplish. You surely have a range of options from working out at a health club, working out at home, walking, jogging, racquetball, group aerobics, sports, weight lifting, swimming, and others. The challenge is to develop a program that meets your health and aesthetic objectives and then to start and sustain the effort. Above all things, you'd wisely select a program of activities that you know you can do and can probably sustain.

Sustaining the effort requires caring about the result, focusing on the process, a degree of discipline (but not a rigid discipline), and a refusal to capitulate to procrastination-process thinking. However, if you relapse, there is an old saying that can help: "If you fall off a horse, get back up again."

Taking and Keeping Weight Off

If there is a far-fetched idea for losing weight, such as sucking in as much air as you can instead of eating, or purchasing tapeworms so you can eat hearty without gaining, somewhere, someone will give it a try. Beyond the ridiculous, a small percentage of dieters are desperate to lose weight and use liposuction, laxatives, diuretics, fasting, purging, skipping meals—practically anything to trim pounds. If someone came from another planet and saw what was happening in the North American culture, that alien would likely have a head-shaking spasm. Our cultural weight-loss fetish appears out of control.

Weight loss and weight control are areas where practically everyone has an opinion. Whole industries have grown to profit from a weight craze that has been with us for decades. The weight industry, however, froths with fads, profiteering, and charlatanism. The macrobiotic diet was once touted as a natural way to eat. Allegedly based on Buddhist yin/yang principles, this diet claimed about nineteen lives in the 1960s. Thereafter, it was associated with child malnutrition. Venfen and herbs like ephedra have claimed lives and sent thousands hurrying to hospital emergency wards. The long-term effectiveness of fad diets and diet pill consumption is unimpressive and the risks are well documented.

Despite hope and good intentions, grabbing on to fad diets has proven to be a high-risk activity. Even when the diet is sensible, diets are artificial. Without positive, long-term changes in eating habits, the relapse rate back to the same or greater weight is unacceptably high. People in this diet pattern put themselves through a documented health risk in their "weight recycling" process. In this area, an empirical approach has merit. A good question for any diet is this: Where is the proof, evidence, or facts that Diet X results in permanent weight loss? What studies appear in peer-reviewed journals, such as *The New England Journal of Medicine* or *Lancet* that affirm the effectiveness of the diet program? Such an analysis can help separate claims from reality. An alert consumer is less likely to be a duped consumer.

Eating healthily has clear advantages that are often overshadowed by aesthetic issues. For example, in Western society, the Rubenesque female form is no longer valued as an icon of beauty. Thin is in. And while males are typically less self-conscious about appearance, at any one time 14 percent diet to lose weight compared with 26 percent of women who are dieters. But those numbers sound conservative compared to the 40 percent of women and 23 percent of men who say they are currently trying to lose weight, but who are generally vague about the form "trying" takes.

Is dieting or trying to lose weight a good thing to do? To say otherwise is like arguing against motherhood, apple pie, and the flag. Yet people who follow fad diets (even legitimate ones) to lose weight face many stresses, and rarely get permanent weight reductions. About 70 percent regain what they lost and more in the year following the diet. Within three years, about 90 percent prefer not to look at the scale. Weight recycling (repeatedly losing and gaining weight) is universal and is not only psychologically discouraging, but can be dangerous to your health. Diets are rarely worth the price.

If you count yourself among those who are dieting in a seesaw weight loss and weight gain pattern, or are "trying" to lose weight, and you want to break from the grim weight-loss statistics, the no-diet plan presents an appealing option. I'll describe this commonsense approach and add the critical component of how to manage procrastination urges to void the discipline that goes with weight maintenance.

The No-Diet Plan

Are you one of the millions who want to weigh within the range considered healthy for your build, height, and age? The no-diet plan is an option. Here is how it works. You decide on a reasonable weight range. You devise a lifetime diet routine that is based on scientifically sound nutritional principles where you consume sufficient calories to maintain your weight at that level. Say you want to weigh 150 pounds and you are now at 180. You figure out the calories you'd need to maintain your weight at 150 pounds. You make sure your average weekly calory consumption is sufficient to maintain a 150 pound weight. Starting the day you have the plan, you execute it. Eventually you'll plateau when your level of consumption meets your body's energy requirements at the weight level you want to maintain.

The no-diet plan is not a quick fix. It is a graduated weight loss process. If you decide to follow this direction, plan to make adjustments as your life circumstances change, but the plan is to continue the no-diet approach. A key advantage of the no-diet plan is this: you no longer need concern yourself with dieting.

Doing the Math

There is no mystery about weight loss math. For approximately every 3600 calories you burn off that you don't replace, you'll lose about a pound. So if your eating habits are stable and you work off an extra 3600 calories a month through exercise, you'll loose about a pound a month. The amount of exercise time to work off a pound can be significant. Perhaps that is why cutting back on calories has appeal. Cutting back 500 calories a day (the equivalent of about four slices of enriched bread) at first looks like an easier route. But for most, this involves a dedication to consistency in self-regulatory behavior and a refusal to capitulate to Wheedler logic. (I'll have more to say about this form of procrastination self-talk later in this section.)

Let's see how weight math works with calorie consumption. Suppose you are a forty-year-old woman who is five feet, five inches tall, of medium build, and weighs 150 pounds. You do moderate exercise, and your routines are comparable to most who are your age. To maintain your weight at 150 pounds takes about 2013 calories a day. To maintain your weight at 125 pounds takes approximately 1939 calories a day. That's not a big difference. A small shift in diet or exercise, over the long run, can make a positive change. But making that difference, as practically anyone who sets on this course knows, is a greater challenge than it first appears. Life is not one big constant, there are many changing variables that can shift a slight balance one way or the other. Start using an automatic dishwasher when you previously washed dishes by hand, and you can throw the numbers off. If you used to burn forty calories a day washing dishes but now use a dishwasher and do nothing different with your diet, you'll likely gain four pounds within a year.

If you prefer to maintain your weight at 125 pounds, then you scale your calorie intake downward to the 1939 range. All things being equal, you'd lose a pound every forty-nine days. But this more patient approach is going to be unrealistic for many. Moreover, dropping seventy-four calories out of your diet can prove challenging, especially if you have a varied diet. So you tell yourself that you want off the weight loss/gain seesaw. The no-diet plan is appealing but too slow. Is there a compromise?

Many compromises are possible. One tradeoff is to start with eliminating 200 calories a day from your diet. Dropping a high caloric item from your diet can serve as a start. If you have two slices of buttered bread a day, dropping both from your regular diet will probably account for more than two hundred calories. If you have three ice-cream cones a week, dropping the ice cream can serve this same purpose.

Instead of the no-diet plan, you could take a rachet-down approach. You set intermediary calorie objectives. You scale down your caloric intake, say, 400 calories a day for six weeks. At that rate, you'd lose a pound about every eight days. Then you stabilize at the 1939 level for six weeks. You repeat the pattern until you reach your goal.

Setting a realistic goal is especially important to the success of your weight-loss and maintenance project. If you start with a reasonable intermediary weight-loss goal, ratchet your weight down, and maintain it for six weeks or more, you may be ready for another goal. An initial goal may be a 5 percent weight loss. Once you've achieved and maintained that goal, you could set another 5 percent weight loss from your now lower weight level. There will come a time where you reach a reasonable plateau. It may not represent your ideal but still represents an empirically justified result. Then you tinker with your diet so that your level of consumption is consistent with your energy needs and thus you can maintain your weight around the 125 pound mark. As you can see, the no-diet approach and rachet-down compromise both involve a strong self-regulatory lifetime commitment to the plan. There is no resting on your laurels if you go this way.

Suppose you are a forty-year-old man who is five feet, ten inches tall, of medium build, who weighs 215 pounds. You do moderate exercise, and your normal routines are comparable to most who are your age. To maintain a 215 pound weight takes about 2730 calories per day. Suppose you decide that you want to get down to 170 pounds, which is comfortably within the preferred weight range of 149 to 182 pounds for a person of your age, height, and body build. Your average calorie intake to balance your energy needs at 170 pounds would be about 2360 calories per day. So you cut your consumption to an average of 2360 calories a day. Following this action and approximately every ten days you'd lose a pound (losing less later as you near your goal). You'd be down to your ideal in between one and two years. Predictably, you'd be at a lower relapse risk.

Motivating Yourself for Change

Some people live into their nineties smoking a few packs of cigarettes a day, leading sedentary lives, drinking a pint or more of vodka a day, and eating junk foods, while repeatedly feeling stressed over imaginary conflicts or being or unfairly disadvantaged.

While the general statistics are against that result, some individuals buck the statistics. But who wants to bet against the odds?

Our nutritional history and habits measurably contribute to health and, perhaps, longevity. Eating healthily can prolong your life and the quality of that life you prolong.

To do the obvious, sometimes you have to tell yourself the obvious. What are the predictable results of an inadequate diet? A nutritionally adequate diet is correlated with reduced health risks for coronary heart disease, cancer, diabetes, cerebrovascular disease, and other dangerous disorders. A correlation doesn't mean certainty. It's a probability statement.

Starting and Sustaining the Effort

Suppose you set as your mission to eat nutritiously in reasonable proportion to maintain your weight at a sensible level in order to gain health and aesthetic benefits. That's a worthy mission for those who stand to benefit from this approach. You may also feel some relief that you don't have to go on another diet. But you will likely face, as part of the challenge, procrastination impulses and procrastination diversionary thinking. But then the odds are that you'd face these challenges regardless of whether you decided on one of the standard commercial, popular, or fad diets or the no-diet way.

Sometimes making minor dietary adjustments is the best strategy. All things being equal, if you gradually decrease, say, feasting on french fries, and replace that with a less fattening and more nutritious alternative, you'll lose weight.

As with any risk-taking and decision-making adventure, you set a weight loss goal and then enter a zone of relative uncertainty. You seek clarity through what you can learn and can accomplish. Let's say that you've developed a sound diet plan and now know the average number of calories to weekly consume so that you gradually get down to your desired weight range. By following a ratchet-down weight-loss goal process, you reach your first goal level, and, let's say, maintain it at that level. Then you adjust your diet and exercise routines so you lose another reasonable amount that you can maintain and still gain a health bonus.

Having plans in place for expected challenges can help you stay motivated. Plan to maintain your benefits through preparing for the worst. How do you handle the virtually inevitable times when you are tempted to add a few extra portions onto a meal, snack between meals, or binge out at holiday times or during lonely periods? How do you handle eating during a crisis period? Although having a plan for high-risk times is no guarantee that you won't relapse, you will have an option.

When you face an untoward situation, and you know you have options, you can choose the procrastination direction or one where you direct yourself to maintain your plan. In my view, having a coping frame of reference for future events is far better than positioning yourself where you think you are helpless to cope because you lack a strategy.

Procrastination-Process Thinking and Weight Loss

You can lose a significant amount of weight then go for years at a stabilized weight. But unusual life circumstances can reactivate old habits. Before you know it, you are ten pounds heavier. How does this happen?

Although Mr. Spock of *Star Trek* fame operated with pure logic, he was a Vulcan. Human beings are psychological. We're an aggregate of primitive urges and intellectually gifted plans that often clash. Emotions can bind reason to a capstan. Logic can give way to bias, and bias can yield to reason. So a straight-line, self-regulatory plan, while logical, would best deal with our individual psychology.

Within the aggregate of our human emotional, psychological, and rational realities, we are impelled to find ways to advantage ourselves, but we also can have strong urges toward a short-term relief that subvert our ability to look beyond the moment. It is here where procrastination can come into play but in a different way than we're used to.

Eating is an action diversion when used to avoid stress. It is also an action diversion when you feel an urge to avoid a displeasure (surprisingly many will drive themselves to consume even when they feel little to no hunger). You can legitimatize this urge by telling yourself something like you'll get back to your no-diet plan later, but for now you need to seize the moment of gustatory delight.

Relapse is a high-probability challenge to practically everyone in whatever weight-loss plan they choose. By treating relapse temptations as a special form of procrastination, you have a wealth of techniques to draw upon. Here are some relapse-inducing conditions that center around Wheedler thinking and some ideas for what you can do about them.

Watch out for the Wheedler. This inner voice is like a flashy lure. The lure appeals, but the hook hurts. You are likely to hear yourself talk in this Wheedler voice when you want to consume for pleasure's sake, avoid a pain of some sort, or try to fool yourself by thinking a single consumptive episode can cause no harm. The compelling pressures from this twisting of the truth lures many to make undone what they pledged to themselves to do. Inner cons such as, "You deserve a break today for all your past good efforts," are pure baloney when your primary goal is to maintain your weight at a preferable level. The voice of the Wheedler can't ordinarily be ignored. Nor is it one that you must obey. So pause, utilize, reflect, reason, and respond approach, to what is in your long-term best interest. After pausing, you can utilize a practical approach, like walking away from a snack table or drinking three eight-ounce glasses of water. Then face the Wheedler challenge by reflecting on the benefits of self-command over a pressured Wheedler urging, or even a mirthful Wheedler ploy, such as "Eat, drink, and be merry, for tomorrow you may die." You can move to a problem-solving mode by focusing on what you have going for yourself that contradicts the Wheedler urges. Perhaps it is a sense of personal pride, a sense of responsibility, a will to prevail, or plain common sense.

Don't let your urges sell you short. You go to a party. You see tasty goodies all around. Although you are really not that hungry, you feel an urge to snack. Indeed, you feel a bit edgy unless you snack. The crackers and cheese, the breaded shrimp, and those tasty cupcakes look irresistible. Like Sirens, they beckon you to the snack table. You tell yourself that this is going to be the last time you do this—tomorrow you'll reform. If you buy this logic, procrastination thinking has hit a homer. The sad part of this scenario is that this is not the end of it. You are more likely to repeat this reaction until you take a stand with yourself. As a prevention technique, create a small card that lists your Wheedler logic. Write a reminder on the card that procrastination thinking is to be expected, but your lifetime no-diet plan is to be respected.

Try not to tempt yourself. You go to a grocery store. As you pick up the staples on your list, you see a friendly bag of potato chips beckoning. It's on sale, and you love sales. You tell yourself that it is a good thing to have snacks available for guests. After all, how else is one to be a good host? As a good host, you add the chips to your basket. Later the bag becomes a source of great temptation. You find yourself in an Apollonion versus Dionysian conflict of the mind against itself. You swing back and forth on whether to eat the chips or leave them. Apollo says no, but Dionysus says go. Next thing you know, you are bargaining with yourself. So you resolve to eat only *one* potato chip. That does sound reasonable. It would end the contest. (Of course, you could trash the bag of chips, and that too would end the conflict.) So you open the bag. After eating one, you tell yourself that the chips are small, and surely another can't hurt. (Who opens a bag of chips and eats just one?) Within a matter of minutes, you are grabbing them by the handful. Then you sooth your Apollonian hackle by saying that once the bag is done, there will be no more to eat. (Note the passive phrases that we often use when excusing procrastination.) Then you say you positively won't buy another bag. (Note the convincing active phrase that we often see when asserting a procrastination decision.) The conflict is done. Think that way, and it's like believing that gazelles can live fearlessly among a pride of lions who nourish themselves by also grazing on grasses. As an alternative, look for where Wheedler thinking first comes into play. The start of the consumptive process begins at the grocery store. Opening the bag is just another step in a predictable sequence of being set up by your Wheedler. The best step is to not buy the potato chips in the first place. Indeed, a good practice is to clear your home of all tempting snacks. If you do intend to binge on chips, go to the gym and work off an equivalent number of calories first. I'll bet if you made exercising off the calories first a precondition for excessive consumption, you'd quickly lose your interest in the binge.

Coasting is not an option. We have to eat to live. We're vulnerable at any time to con ourselves into consuming more, especially if we can convince ourselves that we can get away with it. Sometimes these wishes for eating without consequence can be reactive after years of relative silence. You might, at one point, want to rest on your laurels and tell yourself that you deserve a reward for your years of perseverance. But because you've maintained your desired weight for months or years, that doesn't give you a free pass by Go, as picking the right card in a Monopoly game would do. The weight-math numbers don't change much over the years. It still takes about 3600 calories to gain a pound and about six hours of heavy exercise to burn it off. Forget those numbers, and procrastination-process thinking gains an edge.

Don't buy into the myth. Eating is pleasurable. Restraint is freeing. So we avoid the excesses in a pleasurable form of consumption by restricting both what we eat and the amounts we'll consume. With this freedom by restriction view in mind, you can still eat tasty foods on the no-diet plan. The no-diet is a normal diet, scaled for maintaining yourself at a reasonable weight. So any inner-Wheedler talk of food deprivation is a phony myth. The bottom line is this: you can remain mindful of the boundary conditions you set for yourself on weight maintenance. The restrictions give you the freedom of more opportunities for enjoying your life through reducing the risks and burdens that can come with an overweight condition.

Stress Control

Depending on whose statistics you read, between 25 to 75 percent of people visit their primary care physician complaining of physical symptoms that they don't realize have their origins in stress.

We can define stress in different ways. In one sense, stress is the result of any pressure that disrupts or interferes with our physiological equilibrium (Seyle 1956). A jump in a cold lake on a hot day can do it. An injury can do it. An infection can do it. But when we think of stress, we are more likely to see stress related to negative conditions such as worry, personal conflict, ruminations, confusion, depressive thinking, feeling rushed, facing an unpleasant task, tedious routine, or a buildup of delayed tasks. Beyond our self-induced stresses, disasters, such as a tornado, your best friend betraying you with your mate, or a job loss can evoke an extremely strong and persistent stress reaction.

We are never going to be in a state of perfect equilibrium, so stress is inevitable, even in the most positive of circumstances when you are operating with a realistic and optimistic outlook. Stress can be positive, productive, and propelling and still be destabilizing in the sense that it disrupts our equilibrium. I call this productive stress "p-stress." You experience this disequilibrium when you feel inspired by a problem and put time and drive into its resolution. You may also experience p-stress during and following positive major life events, such as initiating action to relocate to an interesting new area. Even though positive changes produce a disequilibrium effect, that may be just the effect you want to promote.

We pay less attention to stresses brought on by change when we desire those cases. Still, positive change can alter our body chemistry in ways that can sometimes make some of us a bit vulnerable to physical consequences, such as a temporary tendency to be susceptible to the common cold. When such disequilibrium occurs, it can come about from an increase in the hormone cortisol, which has an immune-system-suppressing effect. With some forethought, however, these positive changes are manageable to reduce the minor risk from, say, picking up a cold. Part of this forethought involves mechanical actions. In the cases of relocation, getting familiar with the new territory in advance of leaving the old can be of some help. Maintaining a solid moderate exercise routine helps maintain physical equilibrium.

Persistent worry, depression, or hostility are distresses ("d-stress") that can be quite dramatic. People who chronically feel anxious, for example, experience a highly unpleasant discomfort. Some people with severe panic reactions visit the emergency ward of hospitals many times before it becomes clear that their generally short eruption of heart palpitations, sweating, and hyperventilation involves a physical reaction bathed in panic thinking. D-stress also can be as subtle as it is dramatic, as seen in those who lead inhibited lives where they shelter themselves behind a veil of false securities.

P- and d-stresses exist on different continua. But the continua crisscross. P-stress people tend to mobilize their resources and concentrate their efforts on solving problems. D-stressed individuals are inclined to concentrate on negatives and are more likely to procrastinate. But even the most problem-solving oriented people will have distressful periods of discouragement and procrastination. The most d-stressed folk will have pleasant times, face difficult challenges, and can do well for themselves and others. In this sense, both perspectives overlap, but in degree.

Motivating Yourself for Change

Most people who try to avoid d-stress would prefer a resolution to the problems they avoid. In some cases, they are confused about what is causing it all and don't know where to start.

When you take first steps, you are more likely to feel in charge of yourself and manage the events around you. You are less likely to panic over a negative mood. You are more prone to direct your energy toward managing external events. You are less likely to absorb yourself in festering ruminations or painful inner study where you come to know more and more about your worries and troubles, and less and less about your strengths and capabilities. Is this a sufficient motivation to reach more often for the p-stress option?

Starting and Sustaining the Effort

The old expression "it's all in your head," has some merit but is also misleading. What you think and believe can affect how you feel and how your body functions. For example, people with realistically optimistic outlooks are less likely to get ill than those who habitually stew about frustrated expectations.

When you use stress as a justification for procrastination you delay acting because of an untested hypothesis that whatever you do won't work. Catch-22 strikes again. Catch-22 procrastination is stress activated but does have vulnerabilities that you can address, like those below.

- When caught in catch-22 negativity, it is often difficult to see differently. But life is not static, and thinking is not static. By contrasting static catch-22 procrastination thinking with fluid contradictions, you may find it increasingly difficult to stick with this one-way-thinking formula. For example, consider times where catch-22 didn't apply. What was the difference in your situation and thinking? This juxtaposition can help broaden your perspective to where you can see ways to cope with d-stress.

- When you write out your d-stress thinking, put it aside, then review it a few hours later, you can be better positioned to follow Ellis' ABCDE approach introduced in chapter 8. Using this method, you can cull out your irrational beliefs and start thinking in a *do it now* way.

- The concept of the mental jungle can help define what you are dealing with when you deal with d-stress negativity. Within this jungle you will find many creatures lurking everywhere, clouding the air with thoughts of despair. A frisky monkey throws multiple messages your way. What if you make a mistake—what a disaster. It could be that you are truly inept and can never be otherwise. Don't do anything, otherwise you could be very sorry. A shrieking bird appears from the shadows to tell you that since there is no ultimate solution for overcoming procrastination, there's nothing you can do about it. A snake hands you a magnifying glass so that you can make much out of little. A spider hands you binoculars so you can look from the wrong side and make a lot into a little. A lizard preaches that if you are not "someone," you must be nothing. A puma imparts a thought. "To grow wise," it muses, "you must personalize and generalize." When you catch yourself thinking in these stressful ways, pause and label the thoughts mental jangle-jingle. Labeling a d-stress process is a big step on the path to changing its procrastination-propelling features.

Purging D-Stress with PURRRR

To help yourself halt procrastination stirred by d-stress, combine the PURRR plan from chapter 1 with the ABCDE from chapter 8.

PURRRR PLAN

D-stress procrastination situation: _____

Pause	Utilize	Reflect	Reason	Respond	Revise
Stop to think.	Apply resources to halt diversions.	Activating Event Beliefs Conse-quences	Dispute erroneous negative thinking.	Test *do it now* thinking and actions.	Examine new effects and make adjustments based on feedback.

By acting to purge procrastination from d-stress, you gain a triple advantage. You practice your critical-thinking skills to strengthen them. You can reduce needless stress. You can feel more in command of your life by shifting from a stressful outlook to a *do it now* approach.

Key Ideas and Action Plans

The solution to exercising, maintaining your preferred weight, and reducing needless stress is simple to conceive and can be done with diligence and effort. It involves challenging and curbing negative habits, developing positive proactive habits, and practicing this proactive approach until it dominates. Like most other situations where you challenge procrastination, this effort involves many repetitions of counter-procrastination techniques that you apply to the task. Relapses are part of the script, so have a plan to face them if you intend to maintain your hard-won gains.

What key ideas from this chapter can you use to further you plan to decrease procrastination? Write them down. Then write down the actions you can and will take to support a *do it now* initiative.

Key Ideas

1. _____
_____

2. _____
_____

3. _____
_____

Action Plan

1. _____
_____

2. _____
_____

3. _____
_____

Postscript

Replacing procrastination patterns requires more than a declaration to change, a resolution to change, or using change slogans as mantras. Changing from procrastination to *do it now* patterns typically involves a process. Exercising, weight loss, and stress reduction all involve engaging in a process for positive changes. But such efforts free your time from the results of the procrastination distractions that subvert good health goals. If you want to free more time to have fulfilling experiences, we'll next turn to ways of managing your time to *free* your time.

CHAPTER 14

The Rewards of Time

In ancient cultures, time is measured in seasons. In such cultures, it's important to know when the river floods and to plant crops, or when to migrate before the winter storms. Those with this knowledge hold power. In modern cultures, time has a different meaning. It is a means for regulating our lives as well as a means of measuring our production. There are lunch times, bed times, vacation time, and time to relax. We have schedules and deadlines that define the times to meet responsibilities and social obligations. Were it not for the calendar and clock, the incidence of procrastination would drop.

Our time schedules give us options to predict and take advantage of opportunity. You know, for example, the time for your favorite television show. You know the time it is permissible to leave work. You know the times you can shop at your local grocery store. Were it not for the clock, the occurrence of many events would be unpredictable.

Around the clock in the realm of space, we live our lives. We experience the events that bring us joy, sadness, and our sense of being human. In this time, we stretch our capabilities, deepen our understanding of ourselves, and learn what is important. All this takes place within a subjective inner world of ambiguities, certainties, conflict, curiosity, and confidence.

Time is endless in the sense that we can theoretically relate it to infinity. In our lives, it is not. How we use our limited time reflects the directions we take and the joys or frustrations we experience.

Between the beginning and end of your life, you experience. The question is, what is it that you want to experience that is within your ability to have?

Your Life Line

Procrastination examples abound, but stories and examples of procrastination are like dry words on paper unless you connect them with something of personal relevance. As you look back, how many advantages have you gained by following through on what was important for you to do? Did you complete a desired degree? Did you start work early and leave late to gain a promotion. When you stood up for your rights, did you gain a bit more confidence each time? Have you created valued relationships for yourself? When you felt inhibited to act and still went forward, did you gain a sense of pride by cutting through a tough barrier? Inherent in these proactive efforts, you can find many ingredients for adding to your sense of accomplishment. These are the daily things you do that provide quality content for your autobiography. As you write future autobiographical chapters, what content would you want to include? How about a chapter about how you effectively coped with a tenacious procrastination habit?

Reflections about what you've gained through purposeful actions contrast starkly with losses from inaction. Procrastination propelled by discomfort-dodging motives and drives can leave a trail of regrets, lost opportunities, broken promises, and some especially unfortunate consequences when you "ran out of time."

The graveyard of lost opportunities can be boundless. Have you ever delayed too long declaring your affection for the love of your life, only to see that person walking into the sunset with another? Is there a wrinkled college application lying beneath a pile of unopened magazines? Have you seen a heap of frustrations in the form of incomplete maintenance tasks scattered about as you feel trapped going round and round in a circle of disbelief? Do you periodically get into a flurry of catch-up activities, then fall back to the original pattern of delay? Do you sometimes feel baffled when procrastination spreads to areas that you may have previously enjoyed or could easily do?

What would liberation from procrastination mean in the present and for the future? Are these results sufficiently desirable to use time, expend effort, take risks, and act to defeat procrastination thinking?

Considering the numbers of time-related rules, regulations, and policies we daily follow, you could conclude that overcoming procrastination is a practical process involving the use of time-management scheduling systems. That idea has intuitive appeal.

If we are not mindful of how we use time, we can easily fritter it away. So some time-management plans can be put to use to help structure our time and efforts. But time-management alone is frequently insufficient to decrease procrastination, especially when the procrastination habit process is complicated by personal-development matters such as perfectionism, anxiety, or depression. Indeed, time management is rarely intended as a tool for coping with major life stresses, such as overcoming a painful social phobia. You can, however, schedule yourself for a group for people who want to overcome, say, perfectionism. If you knowingly put that off, then you procrastinate on addressing a correctable problem.

When you use time-management procedures, you act to assert an external control over your time to free up time for other challenging purposes. For example, if you daily face multiple interruptions at your place of work, you can closet yourself in your office for an hour or two a day to work without distraction. This practical solution can give you the advantage of putting effort on your priority activity. The time you're free, you can use in other ways.

Time-management techniques are practical techniques and commonsense actions to make better use of your time. These techniques include listing priorities on cross-out sheets and rewarding yourself for positive actions. They involve creating realistic schedules and sheltering yourself from needless time encroachments. Here are some general tips for getting what you want to do done and saving time.

- Identify and work on your priorities first.

- Continually review your priorities and your progress.

- Modify your system when you can see opportunities to upgrade it.

- Make a start at tackling new priorities as they become evident. Take at least one step. Once you've begun something, it's typically easier to get back to it.

- Manage unexpected non-priority interruptions at a time you set aside for that purpose.

- Set specific times to deal with reoccurring activities. Grocery shopping at 7 A.M. in a nearly empty store is likely to take less time than shopping after work when the store is crowded.

- Make use of mechanical organizing devices such as in-out boxes, electronic schedulers (computer scheduling programs and peripheral devices), and colored file folders (red for top priorities and yellow for the next-in-line priorities).

- Avoid overscheduling yourself. Even if you don't put anything off, you risk falling behind when you have more to do than the time available.

- Keep items you regularly use readily available. For example, if you have a habit of misplacing your keys, set a place aside for them, and get into the habit of putting them in that place.

- A few hours prior to bedtime, lay out what you plan to use the following day: files, materials, clothing, phone lists, schedule, or whatever is needed that you can gather or prepare the night before. This can spare a confrontation with Murphy's Law. (Murphy's Law is the idea that when something *can* go wrong, it will.)

- Throw out recognizable junk mail and other targeted marketing materials.

- Routinely dump old clothing and worn items that you can replace but rarely if ever use. (This keeps the clutter factor down.)

- Take along reading materials for trips on busses, planes, and trains that has information that can help you to get ahead on your prime projects.

- When convenient, use mail order or the Internet to purchase commodity items.

- Get routine documents out of the way by addressing them once. This will help you avoid the paper shuffle.

- Throw off the time hogs. These are time-consuming activities with relatively little return for the time you invest in them. For instance, if you are pressed for time, and have an excessive amount of house cleaning projects, consider delegating them to a family member or hiring a cleaning company for routine cleaning.

- When you have reading material to digest, avoid the perfectionist trap. Focus on getting the gist of the material. Highlight the details for what you want to recall later.

- To jog your memory, use reminder systems for the more critical things you want to remember (to-do lists, e-mail messages to yourself). Avoid cluttering the list with trivial or routine items such as brushing your teeth or feeding the canary.

- Create a pleasant environment for where you do your work at your home or place of work. Pick colors that please you. Have pictures, items, and other paraphernalia that you associate with positive feelings, pleasant memories, and productive outcomes.

- Set process goals. You determine what you need to do to get something done, then you progressively engage the different phases of the process until the task is done.

- Use a reminder system. If you think of something important to accomplish but are legitimately not able to do it now, write yourself a note. Plan to read such notes daily and then *do it now* when you are first able.

- Take a "bits and pieces approach." This is like walking up the rungs of a ladder. Even the most complex tasks have simple beginnings. Break the activity down into "chewable bits" where you can tackle each phase with a reasonable expectation of progress. This method may be particularly useful for projects such as writing assignments, career development, or building self-efficacy.

- Use a cross-out sheet. Here you list your priorities. As you finish each, cross it off the list. Seeing your list dwindle can prove rewarding.

- Create a catch-up, keep-up, and get-ahead organizing system for priority activities. In the catch-up phase, you rid yourself of long put-off tasks. In the keep-up phase, your throw off responsibilities by doing them as they occur. Ultimately you emphasize get-ahead activities where you focus your efforts to achieve priority long-term objectives.

- Complete spontaneously occurring tasks as they arise.

- Do it when you think of it. Memory is fallible. When you think to do something important that you can accomplish now, immediately do it. That way you won't have to recall it at a later time.

If you find that you can boost your efficiency and effectiveness through time-management activities, you'll find shelves of books on organizing and time-management methods.

Key Ideas and Action Plans

To implement this key idea and action-plan approach, list three ideas from this chapter that you believe make the most sense to you in your quest to deal with procrastination. Then write out three actions that you can take to make progress. Let's start now.

Key Ideas

1. _____

_____

2. _____

_____

3. _____

_____

Action Plan

1. _____

_____

2. _____

_____

3. _____

_____

Postscript

There is an old saying that many chop at the branches of evil, but few at its roots. In a parallel sense, attacking the procrastination habit process is like getting at the roots to cut off its nutrients. But whether you go for the branches, roots, or both, your progress will partially depend on how you mobilize your time, self-regulation resources, and effort so that you can use your capabilities more effectively. This process often involves knowing what trail of life you'd prefer to follow, as that helps determine what you find meaningful. We'll visit that domain next, but in an allegorical more than a linear form.

CHAPTER 15

Advancing While Others Procrastinate

It's the procrastinator's basic challenge to stop procrastinating on dealing with procrastination! If you seriously want to get out of a procrastination rut and feel more in charge of your life, you had better consistently work to meet the challenge of getting reasonable things done in a reasonable way within a reasonable time. *The Procrastination Workbook* is an oxymoron of sorts. Here the idea is not so much to play on words, but to contrast the choice. To support a *do it now* choice, the book provides ideas and prescriptive methods you can use to mobilize yourself to develop a powerful inner force for personal change.

The idea for progressively mastering procrastination is simple: You do reasonable things in a reasonable way within a reasonable time. As we have seen, what is simple is not necessarily easy.

Persistent procrastination habit sequences are well-grooved, semi-automatic habit pressures that mechanize a sequence of diversionary activities. The procrastination habit process often has complicating wrinkles, such as when inhibition, depression, and fear color our decisions to promote diversionary actions. When these complicating factors blend with a procrastination process, you'll have to separate them out as part of your work to progressively master procrastination. You will doubtless have many opportunities to practice and strengthen your constructive abilities as you progressively act to supercede procrastination with constructive action. Procrastination is likely to appear at many times and in many guises.

Facing what you needlessly put off is a positive process where you substitute concrete accomplishments for a false hope for a better tomorrow. Clearly, exercising this *do it now* option involves finding effective ways to rebound from lapses to the procrastination process. It also involves persistence. By engaging and re-engaging *do it now* ways of knowing and learning, you load the dice in your favor. What's the alternative? Without direction driven by positive and constructive actions, you are likely to experience frustration without gain.

A higher-level mission can help as a focal point for creating positive experiences for today, tomorrow, and forward until the end of your life. Design a plan to strengthen your mission and follow-through competencies. Execute that plan to achieve more constructive goal outcomes. The key ideas/action plan record that you generated throughout this book gives you a follow-through framework that you can call upon again and again to stir new insight and real personal accomplishments. That's the kind of historical record that can contribute to an interesting autobiography.

What more is there to be said? In this final chapter I'll depart from a structured-change approach and invite you to join me as we look at the p-factor and its solutions through a mythical way of knowing.

Pit an allegorical myth against an academic presentation, and most of us would prefer a wispy fantasy that can give us a new twist to our understanding of everyday experience. Perhaps that is why we are fascinated by stories, and as children, can spend hours listening to many different forms of the tale. A well-told tale says something about life that we sense is right. Moreover, I'd be willing to bet that you remember more about a myth you once heard than a three-hour Chemistry lecture you heard on the same day. So in the remainder of this chapter we'll look at mythical paths of humankind as seen through the eyes of an eagle and a time wanderer. Some paths recognizably tell of procrastination but with an allegorical twist. Thereafter, we'll shift back to the world of reason and logic to explore ways to use the messages we obtain from the paths.

The Myth of the Eagle and Time Wanderer

Once upon a time, not so long ago, two travelers from beyond the farthest horizon of the universe visited the Earth. The first looked like an eagle and was known as Eagle. The second was the Time Wanderer and could take any form it wanted. Although it preferred the forms of a cat, butterfly, or human, the Time Wanderer had the power to move silently and unseen in the form of a mindful breeze or cloud.

Eagle was the visionary who could see the future. From its lofty flight path, it could see all that was happening or ever would be. The Time Wanderer could travel into the past and know the history as well as the present. Moreover, while Eagle could see all that was visible, Time Wanderer could understand what was in the hearts of men and women. Between the two visitors, they could understand all there was to understand about humankind—its past, present, and future.

In due time, Eagle and Time Wanderer came to a high mountain that rose from a broad plain. Eagle flew high and looked at the land below. In this flight, it saw a most interesting sight. At the base of the mountain, Eagle saw five distinctively different pathways worn into the rock of the mountain. It saw the human species on all of the paths. While a few people were struggling to climb the mountain along untouched pathways, a few others followed a narrow, twisting trail. Eagle was amazed to see that most members of the human race were crowded onto three distinctive pathways at the base of the mountain.

Eagle didn't really like flying too close to the ground, so it asked its friend Time Wanderer to find out more about the history of the five paths and of the strange human creatures that it saw.

The quest intrigued the Time Wanderer. With curious anticipation, Time Wanderer joined the people on the different paths, blending in so perfectly that no one realized it wasn't one of them.

The Five Paths of Humankind

The Time Wanderer walked the paths and spoke with the people. It found the travelers on each path to have novel features in their outlook and purposes that separated them from those who trod the other paths. When Time Wanderer had seen all it could see, it went to the tree where Eagle perched and began to tell the story.

"I find each of these paths intriguing," Time Wanderer said. "They are as they have been throughout all of time. Because they looked that way to me, I call them the paths of the Loopers, the Branchers, the Miserable, the Tyrants, and the Voyagers."

Eagle looked pensive. "Tell me what you have seen my friend. I am eager to know more about your discoveries."

The Loopers

The Time Wanderer began by recounting its observations of those who followed the pathway of the Loops.

Scratching its brow, Time Wanderer told its eager friend, "I found a loopy pathway that was crowded with many travelers. People kept going around a deeply rutted roadway. Each had a special track on that path. This is the inertial pathway of life. It is the pathway of routines. People who follow this pathway do little to change the ways of their lives. Some suffer greatly from comparing their lives to their dreams, yielding to their silliest fears, or by living by rigidifying rules that they feel strangled by. The majority of human kind follow that pathway.

"All loopers were not alike. There were those who found pleasure in their routines. These were the maintainers. Their secret lies in taking pride in what they do. Here we find a trash collector who knows all the people on his route by their trash. He takes delight in discovering the changes in people's lives by the changes in the rubbish. We find the physician who works like clockwork in diagnosing and prescribing. Others on this path take good care of their children and routinely show concern about the welfare of their neighbors.

"This path had more than one side. On the ditch along side of the path, millions of Loopers found themselves caught in an endless spiral of sameness. While most perceived the tedium of their section of the path, few showed much enthusiasm for changing it. Fear was their dominant emotion. Their attitude was one of resignation.

"Others mindlessly followed moribund routines and would not bend with the winds that flowed about the trail. Showing an ant-like devotion to routine, they woke each morning, went to work, and did jobs that numbed their minds before limping back home to prepare for the next day. Throughout their lives, day followed day with dreary regularity.

"Another group of Loopers sought a solution to excite their lives. They felt driven to gain prominence or to collect trophies to honor themselves, and they dedicated their lives to this shallow pursuit. This subgroup hoped that prestige possessions would lift a dreary life. However, even with exotic homes and cars, Loopers struggle to evade feelings of ennui that cap a vapid existence.

"Hoards of other Loopers sought passive entertainment to distract them from facing challenges. These spectators observed the lives of others as they fantasized about better times to come. Like sand slipping through their hands, these Loopers felt their lives slip away."

After a pause Eagle said, "I wonder if there is hope for Loopers to ever find themselves?" Blessed with the power of vision, Eagle soared into the sky and looked into the future. Upon returning to the earth, it spoke thus: "I see that most humans will stay on the Path of the Loops. They will know no other experience. A few, however, will leave the path to find their way to experience a more fulfilling life marked by risk and flexibility."

"Yes," said the Time Wanderer. "It has been that way throughout all of the history of this human species."

Eagle said, "I see the future very clearly now. The paths we see today will be in the future as you say they were in the past. The faces change. The world changes. The paths remain the same. There will always be Loopers."

The Branchers

Time Wanderer sat and leaned against a tree and looked at Eagle who was now standing on one leg on a large rock. The Wanderer paused for a moment, then said, "The second pathway had many branches. Most of these led to dead ends. But on this pathway, the travelers tried to discover who they were. They were willing to try anything to obtain enlightenment. They would take any branch on the trail that promised liberation from tedium.

"Branchers had one quality in common. They were normally unhappy, confused, and they felt trapped. Unlike the Loopers, they wanted change, enlightenment, and a sense of meaning.

"This pathway echoed a ring of emptiness, an urgent search for a way to 'be,' and much anxiety. I sensed the great dissatisfaction that members of this group had for themselves and the strong desire to find themselves. Many looked for a master plan that would give meaning to their lives. Others puzzled over how to feel balanced, to experience nirvana, or to have cosmic experiences where they 'merge' with the universe. Some suffered from what their philosophers called an 'existential void': a mental state of meaninglessness.

"A few of the branches on this path led to gurus. The weary travelers who stopped off there hoped to nourish their spirit on the watery gruel of the gurus' cryptic utterances."

With a twinkle in its eye, Time Wanderer narrated, "On one of these side trails, a few of the Branchers found those who promised to share their 'psychic' powers of predicting the future—for a price, of course."

Eagle could not help itself. The creature felt compelled to speak up. "Psychic powers, you say? Only I can read the future. The futures these false seers foretell are not going to happen except through suggestion or chance. Still, I can see these false prophets as far into the future as can be seen. Sorry, my friend, for interrupting you. Please go on."

The Time Wanderer chuckled at its friend's indignation, for it knew that Eagle's feathers were ruffled by false prophecies.

The Wanderer continued, "Some Branchers joined movements. One year they were for saving the earth. The next year they sought new religious experiences. Next, they tried to find life's secrets through meditation, or heal themselves through the magic power of crystals.

"A few believed their present experiences were at least one step removed from life itself. They sought to experience reality in the raw, like hopping on a motorcycle and traveling to new places.

"There were many other side trails Branchers could follow. Some turned to mind-altering drugs or alcohol in order to feel a spiritual high, but they never got to where they wanted to go. Then there were those who lay on the psychoanalyst's couch in the hope that the secret of their future rested in their past. Others believed they had a noble mission, but first they needed to discover what it was.

"You could tell the Branchers by their conversation. They spoke of confusion, gurus, the latest self-help book, religious experiences, existential ideas, and hope. Some spoke of out-of-body experiences. Others spoke of herbs and witchcraft for health and power.

"The path of the Branchers was fascinating. Some members of this group did rise above their existential void and find meaning on this path by discovering values that were guideposts for how to live life, becoming their own guru."

In reflective thought, Time Wanderer said to Eagle, "On the Pathway of the Branches, we find transfer points to the other pathways. But Branchers most frequently crossover to the Loops. Still, some do find a better way."

The Miserable

Time Wander continued, "The pathway of the Miserable was most desolate. There I saw people who distressed themselves by their own demands for comfort and success. Some were passively dependent and insisted they receive what they wanted without effort. Some actively demanded gain without risk.

"The travelers on this path wanted to grab all they could take. They wanted life's gifts handed to them. Spending so much time demanding handouts, they failed to see that they were short-changing themselves because they were taking less than what they could do for themselves.

"Members of this group felt resentful when they did not get what they thought they should have. They lived with the illusion that someone should provide for them. They suffered endless frustration as a result of this illusionary expectation.

"The Miserable talked about what they thought they lacked. They complained about unfairness. Rarely conceding the possibility that they had caused their own problems, they invariably blamed others for their frustrations.

"Some Miserables grew up believing they were little princes and princesses. They assumed the world owed them because they were alive. Instead of changing their perception to fit reality, the Miserable struggled harder to get what they expected through manipulations, coercion, complaining, and cantankerousness. They demanded that others change to make them happy.

"Many sought to smother reality with drugs and alcohol. Others demanded material possessions to fill their inner void.

"The Miserables have opportunities to live a productive life but rarely take the steps to change. Some can improve if they learn to take responsibility for their lives."

Eagle, through its sharp-eyed vision, said, "This group spreads its discontent well into the future. I see with great clarity the visions that line the pathway of the Miserable. Their standards for themselves become progressively lower. With this lowering of standards comes more misery. Those who are going to *expect* less from themselves will progressively *think* less of themselves and demand more and more from others. Unless they change, their future is bleak. They will have no meaningful contribution to leave behind."

The Tyrants

When it arrived at the narrow, twisting path, the Time Wanderer found the trail had a stale but pungent scent and that the path was paved with cold, jagged stones. The creature felt distressed by the history it saw on this pathway. Yet its curiosity was such that it tarried longer on this trail than upon the others. Then, with a heavy heart Time Wanderer told Eagle of its sad insight.

"I saw macabre looking people who dressed themselves in distinctive uniforms to shift attention from their motives to an official image. Their faces were fixed in frozen smiles to project a facade of kindness, friendliness, and cordiality. But their aura was the opposite. They were traveling the Ancient Tyrannical Pathway.

"On this path, I saw people who were psychologically different from the rest of humanity. These are the people who, when they touch you, send a frightening chill through your soul."

The Time Wanderer saw a connection between the tyrants of the past and those of the present. "Independent of time and place," it said, "tyrants were the same. Wherever they went, they destroyed the gladness, joy, and security of the people they touched."

Like a skilled psychologist, the Time Wanderer understood the hearts and the minds of the Tyrant. To its good friend Eagle, it relayed the psychology of the tyrant. "All tyrants are philosophically alike in their hostility toward humanity and in their pathological compulsion to destroy. It starts in this way. The tyrants' head fills with neurotic, destructive insights. Through these insights, the Tyrants develop plans and organize to their desired results. That is their life plan.

"Tyrants engage in a destructive prologue that ultimately ends in defeat. And it is their ultimate wish for their own destruction that is first revealed in their opportunistic and planned destructive acts toward others.

"Tyrants live for control, power, and domination. They have a power pathology. They are like heroin addicts who always need more and more. Their acts become increasingly ruthless as their need to destroy increases. At the pinnacle of their power, they act with unrestrained arrogance. It is here where they are most vulnerable and where they normally self-destruct.

"Some Tyrants first motivate people by love—of an ideal, of a company, of a community, of a country, a religion, or a nationality. Part of the allure of tyrannical leaders is their ability to tap the secret rage felt by the frustrated while cloaking that rage in the dignified uniform of patriotism, idealism, or religion. Here they show a chameleon-like personality to disguise their true motives. They feel most threatened by those who see through the disguise, and are suspicious of all.

"Few travel the Path of the Tyrants. Those who do walk this narrow trail dream apocalyptic dreams of glory through destruction."

The Time Wanderer paused as if in deep reflective thought, then said, "Those with destructive urges have another neurotic insight: through threat, coercion, and intimidation they can control situations and maintain power. Their sense of worth derives from this. Many are good at what they do and so they reapply this destructive talent. Even when discovered, they repeat the pattern because they find their meaning through destruction."

Eagle listened with great intensity. It felt the sadness in the words of its friend. Then it said, "From the sky looking down, I see that Tyrants are the wild cards in the human race. You can't change them, but you can avoid or contain them."

The Voyagers

As Time Wanderer slipped up the mountain slope as gently as a cloud, whose form it now adopted, the creature saw something unusual. Someone was scaling the side of the mountain, climbing higher than anyone else. This human did not follow any particular trail. Sometimes stumbling, sometimes stopping, sometimes thinking of new routes, sometimes building, this Voyager nevertheless kept moving toward the summit.

When the Wanderer looked into the past it saw that Voyagers have been the ones who have discovered, built, and contributed through their creative insights and persistent efforts. The Time Wanderer relayed to the eagle that Voyagers appeared in many forms. The Wanderer saw the presence of a Voyager in Carnegie the industrialist, Lincoln who held a fledgling nation together, and Madame Curie who left a legacy to medicine.

"This constructive creativity takes different forms," Time Wanderer continued. "Voyagers are the gardeners who plant flowers in novel, delightful patterns. They are artists who translate their vision into words, colors, or forms. They are the executives with the vision to translate their resources into productive results. They are the healers who discover new ways to bring others back to health. They are the warriors who protect the innocent.

"Voyagers walk with others and sometimes walk alone. Some create with groups. Some create in isolation.

"Because I was the most curious about this path, I moved in close to take a better look. It was there that I saw a Voyager on the mountain trail."

This creature from beyond the galaxy could see the voyager's glistening sweat, bruised knees, and old scars. It could feel the effort that the voyager made and the pain that the voyager ignored. Thus it said to the Eagle, "I felt amazed at something I felt in the voyager's heart—contentment."

Eagle gave a knowing smile as it related its insightful vision of the future to its friend. "Voyagers bring balance into this world. They stand apart from, yet are part of, humanity. It's this group that gives hope for the future. Their search for truth and their willingness to dedicate themselves to constructive pursuits helps strengthen them and their communities. From this path and from no other do I see hope for humanity."

It was at that moment that both realized the truth of what each saw: When you know the path a person follows, you know about the persons' history, present, and future. But futures can change. Each path intersects with others at different times and in different ways. People can be on more than one path on any given day, and, thus, have choices.

The Trial by Flight

Time Wanderer had a thought and said, "Eagle, why don't we try an experiment? Most of the people I saw are unhappy. Why don't we help them to find their way to the summit? When we get them there, we will find the Voyagers. They all can compare their experiences. Perhaps the Branchers, Loopers, Miserable, and Tyrants will see where their paths lead. Some may choose to join the Voyagers. Others may find ways to contribute and enjoy their lives on the pathway of the loops. Some Branchers may find a way to find meaning. Perhaps a few Tyrants will try a different way."

Eagle thought this sounded like just the thing, then said, "This species is capable of great challenges and changes. I can foresee this. But I'm not so sure about the Tyrants." With that, the golden bird lifted its wide wings and circled the pathways at the base of the mountain. Meanwhile, Time Wanderer adopted the form of a Looper and approached the first Looper it saw.

"Excuse my interruption, friend," Time Wanderer began. "How would you like to go to the top of the mountain?"

"Oh no," the Looper answered. "That mountain is just too steep, and half the trails are in darkness. It's just too dangerous. Besides, I'm tired, and I threw my back out last year playing cribbage. It's an interesting story if you have the time. Anyway there aren't any good guides left. They charge too much. So why bother?"

"Hang on," said Time Wanderer. "My friend will fly you up there. Guaranteed zero risk, no cost, no effort. What do you say?"

"You'll be out of business in no time," said the Looper, "but okay."

Time Wanderer changed form and approached a Brancher in a manner to avoid giving offense. "Friend Brancher," Time Wanderer started in, "how would you like a free trip to the summit?"

"Hey, dude, sounds good to me," said the Brancher, "but do you know if there is a hip mountain dude who knows a secret cave with secret stairs that takes you right there?"

"This is better," said Time Wanderer, taking the Brancher's measure. "No stairs. Just flight. Great view."

"I'm in," said the Brancher.

Then Time Wanderer took the form of a Miserable and approached the first Miserable it saw.

"Excuse me, Miserable," Time Wanderer began.

The Miserable broke in, "Hey I'm in a hurry, weirdo. What do you want?"

"Nothing at all," answered Time Wanderer, beginning to regret the experiment. "Only to offer you a ride to the summit."

"Yeah, well, where's the elevator?" the Miserable demanded. "I was promised an elevator, and I'm not moving until I get what's mine."

"It's better than an elevator," Time Wanderer explained. "My friend the Eagle will take you there, and you don't have to do so much as push a button."

"Well, that's more like it," the Miserable exclaimed. "But I'm warning you—you'd better deliver on your promise."

When the Time Wanderer got to the ancient tyrannical pathway, it said, "Tyrant, would you join us in our rise to the top of this mountain? We have an Eagle transportation service. I'm sure you will find it comfortable."

Without hesitation the Tyrant said, "Of course," then leaped onto the back of Eagle and began to charm the others with wit and visions of a bright tomorrow. "Join me," the Tyrant said, "and I promise you will have everything you want. Look below you and see the kingdom, which you shall rule with me." As the Looper, the Brancher, and the Miserable excitedly looked down, the Tyrant cackled and pushed them off the Eagle.

Eagle swooped and caught the three before they fell. When the Tyrant started tearing at Eagle's feathers, that was too much. Eagle dropped him back on his path, and Tyrant sulked away snarling.

"Wow, that was one bad dude," exclaimed the Brancher.

"I wouldn't want him in my circle," said the Looper.

A visibly shaken Miserable said nothing but wondered why the Tyrant didn't deliver the goods.

When all three were on top of the summit, Eagle and Time Wanderer stood back to observe what would happen. After taking in the view for a short time, they noticed the Voyager by the shade of a bush.

"Did the Eagle fly you up here too?" asked the Brancher, the most curious of the three.

"No," the Voyager said softly, smiling slightly.

"Then how did you get here?" asked the Looper, in amazement.

"I climbed and walked," the Voyager answered simply.

"Wasn't that dangerous?" asked the Looper.

"Not for me," said the Voyager after a moment of thought. "The path felt like the right way to go, and so I did my best to follow it here."

"Did you find the secret stairway, then?" asked the Brancher.

"There isn't any secret stairway," answered the Voyager flatly. "I found the most challenging stairway within me. That I found the hardest to climb."

"How did you climb the pathway you traveled to get here?" asked the Looper.

"With my legs," answered the Voyager with a hearty laugh.

"How did you know what path to take?" asked the Brancher.

"I wasn't sure this was the right way when I began," the Voyager answered. "But once I started, I found I wanted to continue."

"Who carried your luggage?" asked the Miserable.

"My arms," answered the Voyager with another hearty laugh.

"Why did you do it?" the other three asked at once.

"Something within me. I just knew I wanted to go forward, and so I did. On this path I discovered that obstacles are challenges and that I can see new visions once I get beyond them. The possibility of discovery is like a magnet that keeps drawing me toward the summit."

With that, the Voyager turned to scan the horizon, picked up a heavy pack, and started climbing another face of the mountain.

The Looper, Brancher, and the Miserable watched Voyager disappear beyond a rise then realized they were alone.

"Boy, it's sure a long way down," said the Looper.

"I wonder where that Voyager dude went," mused the Brancher.

"I'm not getting any warmer," said the Miserable. "Where the hell's that Eagle?"

Eagle and Time Wanderer were now some distance away at another mountain peak. At that distant spot, Time Wanderer smiled a knowing smile.

"Why are you smiling?" asked Eagle.

"It's the irony of it all," said Time Wanderer. "Any of them could, like the Voyager, get to the summit on their own—practically at will. They don't realize that the summit is a process. Yet you, my friend, are frowning. What's troubling you?"

"I'm looking into the future," said Eagle. "And I'll say no more except that the path of the Voyager is the one place to travel, but few will ever find it." With that, the Eagle carried the three travelers back to their paths.

How to Use the Paths

Only a courageous few break the magnetic pull of the pathways of the Loopers, the Miserable, and the Branchers to walk with the Voyager. Sadly, Tyrants practically never walk the Path of the Voyager.

In a practical sense, it is the rare person who only walks one path. While most people spend time on each path, they dwell on one more than on the others. The characteristics of that path give definition to their lives. Because you can find the same person on different paths at different times, you cannot always tell their dominant path. A Tyrant, for example, may appear at one time to follow the Path of the Miserable. You may discover, to your surprise, that when you travel beside this person, your world feels unstable and insecure.

What happens if you want to cross over to the Path of the Voyager, or to follow enjoyable routines, or to find meaning in your life? For those who seek meaning, enjoyment, and to make contributions, here are some maps for your travels.

Philosophical, compared with the earlier chapters of the book, this chapter describes crossing the bridge from one of the procrastination pathways to one of purposeful action. There will be four prime ways to accomplish this shift. One relates to the personal experience of Ben Franklin, a second to the scientific approach of psychologist George Kelly, the third to the views of Jean Payot, and the fourth involves a philosophical *I ching* perspective. Then I'll describe my perspective for what it takes to cross the bridge to the Path of the Voyager.

Franklin's Model Person

Near the end of the eighteenth century, American diplomat Benjamin Franklin wrote his *Autobiography* (1989). In it, he explained how to make a "self" for fun and profit. Using his life as a model, he drove home one central idea: develop the attractive qualities of your *real self*.

Here are some of the specifics of Franklin's observations and advice.

- Recognize the fluidity of situations. They constantly change.

- Your model self will operate in a field of many less capable competitors.

- Appearance often counts more than self-discovery.

- We earn character and credit by hard work. Avoid all demeanor to the contrary.

- Maintain a sense of detached curiosity or wonder at the elements of human nature. This posture increases your chances of controlling the actions of others.

- Recognize that you can manipulate people by what they regard as being in their interest. You can confidently and honestly play on other people's motives.

- Project yourself as an arbitrator. Show people how to join together to promote their common interests. To do this, remove all personal prejudice and remain free of it.

- Express yourself with "modest diffidence." Avoid the use of terms like "certainly," "undoubtedly," or any other term that gives the air of positiveness to an opinion. Rather say, "I conceive or apprehend a thing to be so and so, it appears to me, I imagine it to be so."

- Practice truth, sincerity, and integrity in dealing with people.

- Discover yourself by practicing positive values.

Franklin said he practiced the virtues of resolution, temperance, order, industry, sincerity, moderation, and tranquility. For resolutions he noted: "Perform without fail what you resolve." For tranquility he says to not feel disturbed "at trifles or by accidents common or uncommon."

He took his ideas seriously. He used worksheets to record experiences. He used numbers and charts to measure his progress. These worksheets are similar to those that behavior therapists use today to measure their clients' progress. Through his book, Ben Franklin established himself as America's first personal-change self-help author, and perhaps its first behavior therapist.

Franklin tells us he never arrived at perfection especially about orderliness (keeping items in their place). He tells us, "Yet I was by this endeavor a better and happier person than I otherwise should have been if I had not attempted it."

Ben Franklin strove to act like a model person. His efforts paid dividends. He made important contributions as a scientist, thinker, and diplomat. Still, by his admission, he was not perfect. In Franklin's world, different conditions may require different responses.

Like Franklin, you will never overcome all limitations and faults. You will never actualize all your potential. Yet, as you strive to build a model *you*, you can make significant gains. You can go farther than you have traveled before and you may enjoy the trip.

Kelly's Model Person

Psychologist George Kelly's Role Construct system (1955) complements Franklin's ideas. In the 1950s, Kelly shed light on how to build a model person. He tells us to play different roles to discover what we can do.

This is how Kelly's system works. Begin by devising new roles you can play that can help you build your positive attributes. List the attributes you want to build. They can be anything, including becoming an active listener, a conflict manager, more easygoing, meticulous, confident, imaginative, venturesome, or persistent.

To start, pick one attribute you want to develop. Write an advertisement for yourself that highlights that attribute. Create a script around the attribute. Plan the scenes. Pick your nonverbal activities. Decide where to play out the role. Decide how long the scene will be. You can always change the scene, time, and content once you start. Then give your character a name that suits the part you plan to play and keep it to yourself. Test out your role in the real world.

If you're not sure what to do, take on the role of a person who uses *aspiring* words such as "prefer," "want," or "desire." These terms crowd out *requiring* words such as "expect," "demand," or "insist." Requiring ways create inner tension.

When you think in aspiring ways and take on new roles, you may find that the language you use to express yourself will reflect these new positive actions. You may also

---

Although you can never achieve perfection,
by striving for excellence you can achieve beyond the ordinary.

> Testing promising new behaviors can feel clumsy at first.
> However, when you start to get positive feedback for
> these efforts, you are likely to want to repeat what works.

find yourself using active verbs to foretell your actions. Active verbs seem to be associated with a *can do* attitude.

Kelly does not suggest that you develop a practiced phoniness. His idea is to help you break negative patterns by testing out new behaviors that compete against the negatives.

Kelly believes that when we play different roles, we learn more about ourselves. Still, this type of change is like wearing new shoes. It can feel uncomfortable until you have walked in them for a bit.

The Will to Change

Franklin tells us to pick attributes we want to develop and practice developing them. Kelly tells us to test them in the roles we play. French educator and psychologist Jean Payot (1893) says we need to assert our *will* to change for the better. Payot thought that will, effort, and sweat nourish the taproot of change.

Payot wrote that strenuous and persistent efforts, unless directed, are not enough. To make a worthwhile effort we would wisely seek a direction and work toward some important end. When you do this, he says, "ideas and work will draw nourishment from everything." Here are some of his observations:

- We fuse the bonds between ideas and conduct "by the heat of emotion." He correctly implied that emotionally charged ideas motivate action. What we think, the way we feel, and what we do bind together. By implication, when we change one part of the trilogy, we change the other two.

- People who spend their time undermining other people's efforts waste their energy. It's far wiser to work to accomplish something meaningful.

- Our minds fill with ideas that contradict one another, and often we don't see the incongruity. The implication is that multiple perspectives are possible within each of us.

- "The smallest evidence of fact will always outweigh authority." Search for the facts, look for evidence, and avoid thoughtless acquiescence to official-sounding statements.

> The Olympiad Charter presents the idea of fashioning
> "a life based on the joy found in effort."

The *I Ching* Perspective

We can reframe reality through paradoxes and see our lives from a different perspective. When you change your views to fit a reframed reality, you have experienced a radical change in perspective. The *I ching* or Chinese Book of Changes offers ideas you can use to help yourself reframe your views about procrastination.

The *I ching* contains sixty-four named hexagrams, aphorisms, and accompanying interpretations. Here are two of the aphorisms that relate to procrastination and time: "Do not expend your power prematurely in an effort to attain, by force, something for which the time is not right." "In the chaos of the beginning, order is already implicit." When you look beyond the mysticism of this text, you can see the merit in the ideas of the ancients who authored this book of change. Consider:

- To grow wise and to contribute requires accurate timing and pacing, along with love, patience, perseverance, creativity, and receptivity. It is not possible to achieve everything at once.

- Time is not a barrier but the medium for actualizing potential.

- When there is difficulty in the beginning, your struggle gives meaning to what transpires.

- When hindrances happen, patience is often the answer. An unlikely event may happen to help clear the path. If you feel blocked, you may need to stand back to see where the power to transcend lies.

- At the time of a standstill, you are nearing the point of change into its opposite. Times of darkness pass. Times of decay end. The hero or sage within you returns to power.

- As you examine yourself, measure the effects your actions produce and consider alternatives if your actions fail.

- If you are to lead others, you must first objectively judge yourself.

Crossing the Bridge

Crossing the bridge to the Voyager's path involves a radical change in perspective. Here you have to keep your mind open to new solutions to old problems and old solutions to new problems.

As you cross the bridge, keep aware of changing peripheral conditions. Concentrate on what you are doing. Act this way, and you are on a pathway that is radically different from the one that most others follow.

You can take comfort in knowing that you have sound resources. You can design a model person and strive for that ideal of excellence using these resources. You can't be sure you will triumph in the end. Still, as Ben Franklin learned, he was better off making the effort than in not trying. Perhaps that part of your autobiography will read the same as his. Try experimenting with radical changes in perspective, and see.

The Radical Change in Perspective Involves Changing

From	To
Demanding success	Willingness to risk failure
Constraints	Freedom
Crisis	Opportunity
Finding oneself	Discovering resources
Internalization	Experimentation
Risk avoidance	Risk management
Reducing malfunctioning	Expanding functioning
Need fulfillment	Goal attainment
Old boundaries	New insights

Key Ideas and Action Plans

The allegorical Eagle and Time Wanderer myth illustrates ways to substitute purposeful action for procrastination. Through this myth, we traveled five paths and looked for ways to cross over from those that lead to misery to those that hold hope for taking charge of your life today and for the days to come. But the Voyager's path we see among the human trails is not a quick nor an easy path to take, nor is it practical for everyone to take. There can be no guarantees that the Voyager's path will lead to where you want to go. But on that path, or a selective modification of it, you can find opportunities, create valued experiences, and develop a realistic hope for present day and future fulfillment through the power of your efforts.

Is the myth memorable enough to cause a measurable shift in perspective away from procrastination habit-pattern sequences to problem-solving sequences? There are personal as well as scientific ways of knowing that apply. If, in a personal way, the myth causes you to incubate some more on your future, and you find yourself accomplishing more with fewer needless distractions, then the myth serves its intended purpose. It may also be that shifts can be explained by a combination of other factors and forces. If you do better, the "whys" are of interest, but the actions are more important.

What key ideas from this chapter can you use to further you plan to decrease procrastination? Write them down. Then write down the actions you can and will take to support a *do it now* initiative.

Key Ideas

1. _____

_____

2. _____

_____

3. _____

_____

Action Plan

1. _____

_____

2. _____

_____

3. _____

_____

Postscript

Few things in human psychology are fixed. What we know about procrastination continues to grow. The research is turning up new understandings. I'm learning something new about the p-factor every day, and I've been writing and working in this area for thirty-two years at the date of this publication. With that, we've come to the end of *The Procrastination Workbook*. But the end is a new beginning for something else. What that something else might be, only you can foresee through developing clarity, sharpening your direction, and enjoying your experiences. In that spirit, here is one final thought:

> *The threads of life are thin and strong.*
> *At first, we see them go on and on.*
> *But with the movement of the clock,*
> *The threads unravel and we are lost,*
> *Like pictures etched in frost.*
>
> —Dr. Bill Knaus

We have limited time to learn, contribute, and enjoy our lives. But this pathway to fulfillment is open to those who risk using their time and resources wisely.

References

Aurelius, M. 1964. *Meditation*. New York: Penguin.

Ausubel, D.P. 1963. *The Psychology of Meaningful Verbal Learning*. New York: Grune and Stratton.

Barron, K.E., and J.M. Harackiewicz. 2001. Achievement Goals and Optimal Motivation Testing Multiple Goal Models. *Journal of Personal Social Psychology* 80:706–722.

Borgh, J.R., and T.L. Chartrand. 1999. The Unbearable Automaticity of Being. *American Psychologist* 54:462–479

Davis, M., E.R. Eshelman, and M. McKay. 2000. *The Relaxation and Stress Reduction Workbook*. Oakland, Calif.: New Harbinger

Deci, E.L., R. Koestner, and R.M. Ryan. 1999. A Meta-analytic Review of Experiments Examining the Effects of Extrinsic Rewards on Intrinsic Motivation. *Psychological Bulletin* 125:627–668

Ellis, A.E. 1994. *Reason and Emotion in Psychotherapy: A Comprehensive Method of Treating Human Disturbance*. New York: Carol.

Ellis, A.E., and W.J. Knaus. 1979. *Overcoming Procrastination*. New York: New American Library.

Ferarri, J.R., and T.A. Pychyl, eds. 2000. Procrastination: Current Issue and New Directions (Special Issue) *Journal of Social Behavior and Personality* 15:1–338.

Frankl, V. 1998. *Man's Search for Meaning*. New York: Washington Square Press.

Franklin, B. 1989. *The Autobiography and Other Writings*. New York: Bantam Books.

Gallagher, R.P., A. Golin, and K. Kelleher. The Personal Career and Learning Skills Needs of College Students. *Journal of College Student Development* 33:301–309.

Harriot, J.L., and J.R. Ferrari. 1996. Prevalence of Procrastination Among Samples of Adults. *Psychological Reports* 78:611–616.

Heimpel, S.A., J.V. Wood, M.A. Marshall, and J.D. Brown. 2002. Do People with Low Self-Esteem Really Want to Feel Better? Self-Esteem Differences in Motivation to Repair Negative Moods. *Journal of Personality and Social Psychology* 62:128–147.

Homer. 1992. *The Odyssey.* New York: Knopf.

Wilheim, R., trans. 1962. *I Ching.* Princeton, NJ: Princeton University Press.

Kelly, G. 1955. *The Psychology of Personal Constructs.* New York: Norton.

Knaus, W.J. 2000. *Take Charge Now: Powerful Techniques for Breaking the Blame Habit.* New York: John Wiley and Sons.

———. 1998. *Do It Now: How to Break the Procrastination Habit.* New York: Wiley and Sons.

———. 1982. The Parameters of Procrastination. *Cognitive and Emotional Disturbance,* edited by R. Greiger, and I. Greiger. New York: Human Sciences Press.

———. Procrastination, Blame, and Change. *Journal of Social Behavior and Personality* 15:153–166.

Mayer, R.E., J. Heiser, and S. Lonn. 2001. Cognitive constraints on multimedia learning when presenting more material results in less understanding. *Journal of Educational Psychology* 93:187–198.

Miller, T.Q., T.W. Smith, C.W. Turner, M.L. Guijarro, and A.J. Hallet. 1996. A Meta-analytic Review of Research on Hostility and Physical Health. *Psychological Bulletin* 2:322–348.

Payot, J. 1893. *The Education of the Will.* New York: Funk and Wagnals.

Sagan, C. 1997. *The Demon Haunted World.* New York: Ballantine.

Schachter, D.L. 2001. *The Seven Sins of Memory.* Boston, MA: Houghton Mifflin.

The Columbia Directory of Quotations. 1998. New York: Columbia University Press.

Selye, H. 1956. *The Stress of Life.* New York: McGraw-Hill

Tice, D.E., E. Bratslavsky, and R.M. Baumeister. 2001. Emotional distress takes precedence over impulse control: If you feel bad do it! *Journal of Personality and Social Psychology* 80: 53–67.

Todd, M.Q., T.W. Smith, C.W. Turner, M.L. Guijarro, and A.J. Hallet. 1996. A meta-analytic review of research on hostility and physical health. *Psychological Bulletin* 119:322–348

William J. Knaus, Ph.D., is a licensed psychologist with more than thirty years of clinical experience and research specializing in procrastination and its treatments. As a preeminent expert in this area, Knaus has conducted scores of workshops and groups for procrastinators, has been a guest on *Good Morning America*, and has been interviewed for articles in *U.S. News and World Report, Self, The New York Times, The Washington Post*, and *The Chicago Tribune*. Knaus is former Director of Training at the Albert Ellis Institute for Rational Emotive Behavior Therapy. He is the author of several best-selling books, including *Do It Now!* and *Overcoming Procrastination* with Albert Ellis.

Foreword author, **Albert Ellis, Ph.D.,** is the founder of The Albert Ellis Institute for Rational Emotive Behavior Therapy, which has affiliated centers around the world. He has written more than 50 books and 700 articles, including the best-selling *Overcoming Procrastination, A Guide for Rational Living*, and *How to Stubbornly Refuse to Make Yourself Miserable about Anything—Yes, Anything*. He is currently the President of The Albert Ellis Institute in New York City.

Some Other
New Harbinger Titles

The End of-life Handbook, Item 5112 $15.95

The Mindfulness and Acceptance Workbook for Anxiety, Item 4993 $21.95

A Cancer Patient's Guide to Overcoming Depression and Anxiety, Item 5044 $19.95

Handbook of Clinical Psychopharmacology for Therapists, 5th edition, Item 5358 $55.95

Disarming the Narcissist, Item 5198 $14.95

The ABCs of Human Behavior, Item 5389 $49.95

Rage, Item 4627 $14.95

10 Simple Solutions to Chronic Pain, Item 4825 $12.95

The Estrogen-Depression Connection, Item 4832 $16.95

Helping Your Socially Vulnerable Child, Item 4580 $15.95

Life Planning for Adults with Developmental Disabilities, Item 4511 $19.95

Overcoming Fear of Heights, Item 4566 $14.95

*Acceptance & Commitment Therapy for the Treatment of Post-Traumatic Stress Disorder &
     Trauma-Related Problems*, Item 4726 $58.95

But I Didn't Mean That!, Item 4887 $14.95

Calming Your Anxious Mind, 2nd edition, Item 4870 $14.95

10 Simple Solutions for Building Self-Esteem, Item 4955 $12.95

The Dialectical Behavior Therapy Skills Workbook, Item 5136 $21.95

The Family Intervention Guide to Mental Illness, Item 5068 $17.95

Finding Life Beyond Trauma, Item 4979 $19.95

Five Good Minutes at Work, Item 4900 $14.95

It's So Hard to Love You, Item 4962 $14.95

Energy Tapping for Trauma, Item 5013 $17.95

Thoughts & Feelings, 3rd edition, Item 5105 $19.95

Transforming Depression, Item 4917 $12.95

Helping A Child with Nonverbal Learning Disorder, 2nd edition, Item 5266 $15.95

Leave Your Mind Behind, Item 5341 $14.95

Learning ACT, Item 4986 $44.95

ACT for Depression, Item 5099 $42.95

Integrative Treatment for Adult ADHD, Item 5211 $49.95

Freeing the Angry Mind, Item 4380 $14.95

Living Beyond Your Pain, Item 4097 $19.95

Transforming Anxiety, Item 4445 $12.95

Integrative Treatment for Borderline Personality Disorder, Item 4461 $24.95

Depressed and Anxious, Item 3635 $19.95

Is He Depressed or What?, Item 4240 $15.95

Cognitive Therapy for Obsessive-Compulsive Disorder, Item 4291 $39.95

Child and Adolescent Psychopharmacology Made Simple, Item 4356 $14.95

Call **toll free, 1-800-748-6273,** or log on to our online bookstore at **www.newharbinger.com** to order. Have your Visa or Mastercard number ready. Or send a check for the titles you want to New Harbinger Publications, Inc., 5674 Shattuck Ave., Oakland, CA 94609. Include $4.50 for the first book and 75¢ for each additional book, to cover shipping and handling. (California residents please include appropriate sales tax.) Allow two to five weeks for delivery.

Prices subject to change without notice.